Lake Fly Fishing Guide

By Jim Bradbury
and
Beverly Miller

Frank Amato

PORTLAND

Dedication

To my wife, Joyce and Bev's husband, John for having more understanding than I think I would. Thanks Joyce. Thanks John.

Acknowledgments

Jim Bradbury would like to say thanks to the following people:

Tom: the man who taught me to tie more than just one fly and then take it fishing

Doyle: who taught me about the chironomid

Jim: for letting me play in his pond

Rick: who taught me how to fish the *callibaetis* nymph

Some guy I don't know: for giving me a copy of the Hosmer Minnow

Bev: for all the laughs and for making me realize that there is more to float tubing than catching fish.

And thanks to all of the beginners I've fished with. I have a set of rules I fish by, beginners don't have rules. They made me do things I had never thought of and fish flies I would never have tried.

So thanks to all for making float tubing such a great joy for me.

At this time Beverly Miller wishes to thank her husband and best friend John, who hates to fish, for supporting her rather expensive fishing habits and understanding her need to go fishing almost every day of the week. Without the help of family and friends she could never have struggled through learning how to use a computer in order to write this book. Special thanks to all of her children and her brother John Needham for their assistance in her efforts. Thanks also go out to the Forest Service for allowing us to publish their free handouts of the Mount Hood National Forest lakes.

Copyright 1994 • Jim Bradbury & Beverly Miller
Book Design: Charlie Clifford
Map Drawings: Bill Herzog
Fly Photos: Jim Schollmeyer
Cover Photo: Beverly Miller
Back Cover Photo: Richard T. Grost

Printed in U.S.A
Frank Amato Publications
P.O. Box 82112 • Portland, Oregon 97282
(503) 653-8108 • Fax: (503) 653-2766
ISBN: 1-878175-72-6
10 9 8 7 6 5 4 3 2 1

The Authors

Jim Bradbury

It didn't take Jim long to discover that there were no large trout (over five pounds) in the Clackamas or Sandy rivers. So in 1984 Jim turned to the high lakes and on his first trip to Round Lake Jim learned that he could not reach the rising fish from the bank. He needed a tool and that tool was a float tube. Between April and December Jim averages 3 or 4 days a week in his float tube. Jim says, "Take up float tubing, it's the greatest thrill you can have." Jim's claim to fame is the Bradbury Jig.

Beverly Miller

Beverly Miller is a native Oregonian and even though she grew up around a father who loved to fish she was never really interested or had time for the sport until her fifth child was almost ready to leave the nest. At this same time her daughter and son-in-law moved to a house on the Clackamas River. Gaining confidence in this safe environment she trucked on up the Clackamas River fishing as often as she could with her children Leslie, Dan, Steve, John and Ben. One fateful day on the river she asked a stranger, (Jim Bradbury) if he ever caught fish using his bobber and jigs. Those words and his reply of "Come on, I'll show you and your son how," led her into a rewarding fishing relationship with Jim. With one memorable trip to a lake she found her fishing niche and knew that fly fishing lakes was where her body and soul wanted to be. No more boredom, as each new lake is always an exciting challenge

The Silver Dream

Rainy days of winter fill the swollen stream
And now the murky waters obscure my silver dream.
Angry torrents pass, over jagged rocks
Cold penetrates my waders and even woolen socks.
Fingers numbed by ice, reactions slowed by pain,
It's hard to reel line in and cast it out again.
No fish for me this day as I shiver in this spot
Standing in a frigid stream that harbors fish uncaught.
Bickering Jays chase off a Hawk, they make an awful fuss.
A startled deer bolts, from thick brown underbrush.
With steaming coat and labored breath he loudly races by,
While birds land in the Douglas Fir with a triumphant cry.
The elusive fish is hiding and exactly where, I can't discern
Yet the silver dream is but one reason, I'll hasten my return.

—Beverly M. Miller

An acquaintance of mine enjoyed fishing for steelhead on the Clackamas River. Her stories about fishing experiences coupled with my own, inspired me to write this poem. I will never forget her elation when she caught her first winter steelhead—nor mine!

Contents

Introduction

On our way home from a fantastic day catching fish, we were driving along the road reliving each moment of fun and success we had achieved during the day. (It always takes a good hour before our fishing high is on the decline.) In our high and weakened state of mind it occurred to us that it would be great if other fly fishermen could capture the same pleasures we found in fishing our lakes. We entertained this idea as well as discussing the disclosure of "well guarded fishing secrets." The decision was simple: if our lakes ever get too crowded, we will go find new ones to fish. End of discussion! We both felt our information about fly fishing specific lakes could open new doors to the fishing community. We wouldn't mind seeing another fly fisherman on our favorite lakes catching and releasing fish, having as much fun as we do. From this fragment of an idea a book was born.

One of the greatest fly fishing experiences you will ever have is to catch a fish on a dry fly. There is nothing like it and we advocate fishing dry flies when the time is right. If you want to catch "lots of fish all day long" you will need to fish with wet flies or nymphs. We fish nymphs about 90 percent of our fishing day, saving the other 10 percent for the great "dry fly experience." Nymph fishing is a productive way to catch fish the entire day.

We have written this book for the novice as well as experienced fly fishermen. You will discover that it doesn't take an expert to catch fish with a weighted nymph on a fly line. After reading our book we hope to see you on our lakes catching fish on nymphs from your float tube.

With a float tube you will enter a private fishing world that requires no cumbersome boat trailers, hitches, motors or special boat licenses. You may fish any lake your car and legs can carry you to by simply packing your tube, rod and fins on your back. Fish, camp, fish, eat, fish and then go home when you are too exhausted to fish anymore. In case you didn't know, home is the place where you need to rest to prepare to go fishing again! Now we do feel obliged to warn you: after your first trip you will undoubtedly become a float tube addict. We promise that this will be a beneficial addiction. It will permit you to develop a special relationship with nature and the old skills of observation and listening will take on fresh meaning as you tune in to a new outdoor radio station. Raindrops splashing on water, singing birds, wind shaking the leaves of trees as it pelts you with a hatch of tiny thumping bugs. A twig snapping under the weight of a wild animal, fish slurping up spent insects, the sound of the wind whistling through the wing feathers of flying ducks. These are but a few surprises waiting for you as you sit in a float tube. A float tube definitely offers you a great opportunity to discover new sights and sounds, two keys to unlocking the secrets of catching fish in any lake.

Besides the geographic location you will find that each lake is different. We can almost guarantee that several of our lakes will become your favorite fishing places. It is our goal that you should be able to go to any lake that has an insect hatch, tie on a nymph resembling what is hatching, and using our nymph techniques and retrieves catch fish. By doing nothing more than what we describe even a non-fishing person can catch fish on a fly. If you can buy or borrow a float tube, hold a rod in your hand and kick your feet you have the qualifications needed to fly fish from a float tube. There is no secret society to join and no sacred oath to take. It is simple; just go do it!

Forget Casting!

When you are fishing from a float tube it is not necessary to cast the line from your rod unless you want to or know how to. Assuming that you are a novice and have chosen not to cast you will still need to enter the water in your tube, sit down and begin by attaching the nymph of your choice to the tippet. Kicking backwards with your flippers you may drop your fly into the water in front of you and release the desired amount of line into the water by pulling line off the reel with the hand not holding the rod. This method will work for all types of lines. If, for example, you have chosen to fish with a sinking line, slow your kicking down to a crawl allowing time for the line to reach the desired depth. After you have released the right amount of line and it is at the depth you want to fish you may start the retrieve or line twitch. You may want to barely kick your fins as you retrieve the line or you may want to race across the water. The kick and retrieve will depend on what type of nymph you are fishing as well as the lake and time of year.

The information on how to fish individual flies will be covered in the Fly Pattern chapter of this book. The method that we have described above should replace the need for casting for anyone who feels unqualified. This system works! A novice, handicapped or lazy person can catch fish in this manner; we have proved it over and over.

We haven't said that casting would not expedite the process of placing the fly in front of a fish. This is especially true when you are fishing a floating line and want to cast to one particular fish. I recall one awesome day at Rainbow Lake when a friend who had never fly fished caught 20 fish using our nymph techniques. On the other hand, another friend who has fly fished for years fished with us at this same lake. This guy's casting was art in motion but he only caught one fish the entire day. Upon arrival at the lake he quickly noticed a few fish surface feeding and knew that dry flies should work. (The fish had already tried this trick on us.) We attempted to share our knowledge with him but he couldn't let go of what he thought should work. He watched us catch fish during the day using our nymph techniques with very little casting but he stubbornly did things his way. His one fish day was okay by us! In all honesty we find that on an average most beginners can hook at least three to six fish on their first outing. Of course, there will always be exceptions to every rule. Stop at Hagg Lake and fish for perch in late summer when the water is low and you may exceed a 20 fish day.

Returning to the subject of casting, if and when you decide to learn how to cast we suggest that you invest in a fly casting video. There are many good videos on the market. If we tried to tell you exactly how to develop casting skills in this book it would take volumes of words and you would still find it extremely difficult to visualize our instructions.

Rods, Reels and Lines

*J*im's first rod was a very inexpensive piece of equipment. He assures me that he took more fish with that rod than I would ever believe. Then a stranger rode into town and said, "Here, why don't you try my rod?" Familiar story? Soon his old faithful rod was hidden away in the back of a closet and Jim was sporting a new expensive 9-foot rod. This story almost made me weep. I was feeling mighty sorry for that old rod which could have something to do with my age and symbolism.

The story also serves to remind me that in a marriage where a fishing person is attempting to live in harmony with a non-fishing spouse, it often becomes necessary to justify a few fishing purchases. Large purchases like fly rods, reels and lines can take an obvious bite out of the lunch or grocery money. I love the knowing look in a non-fishing person's eye when my justification tactics begin. Here are some ideas that might work for you:

1. I have tendonitis in my elbow and the doctor thinks a graphite rod will alleviate the pain.

2. With a lighter rod I will get better gas mileage and save you

money.

3. With a new rod and reel fishing trips will be shorter because I'll catch all the fish more quickly.

4. With an expensive lighter rod I'll have energy left over at the end of the day to do more work around the house.

5. Did you realize that this rod was designed to strengthen the arm muscles I use when I mow the grass?

6. I had to buy new fly line because I ran out of line on the Weed Eater and substituted my old fly line.

7. I need a new reel and line because I used the old one for walking the dog.

8. I need a new float tube. You don't want me to drown do you? (I worry when there is no response to this question.)

Let's talk rods! You are going to find that rods come in different lengths, strengths and weights. There is a fly rod made for every fishing occasion. There is a rod designed for playing the smallest of fish to the largest. A small fish on a light fly rod can feel like you are bringing in a whale. Naturally you wouldn't want to fish for small lake perch with a fly rod that was heavy enough to hold and play a Chinook salmon. Choose the rod for the type of fishing you are going to do and size of fish you plan to catch. For the lakes we fish a 5 or 6 weight rod is more than adequate.

A few years ago fiberglass rods were "in." They were strong, flexible, slightly heavy and popular. We discovered that on a few models you would need a build like Walt the professional wrestler in order to set the hook while other models were perfect for fishing dry flies. There are many people who enjoy fishing with their fiberglass rods and wouldn't change rods for anything. Graphite is now part of the fishing scene. We happen to have a personal preference for graphite or a graphite composite rod. The rods are strong and lighter than ever. There is a fly rod out that weighs one ounce.

The rod progression reminds me a little of the tennis racquet industry. Remember when wood racquets were in? Then along came new materials and innovations that actually made the player look as if he could play better. Jim and I both enjoy trying out new products and some do work better than the old timers. You can bet I'm not throwing away my old wood tennis racquet any more than I would toss a bamboo fly rod! You will find that the graphite rods seem to have the same amount of bend throughout the entire rod allowing more of the rod to work the fish. We recommend you begin with a rod of medium flexibility. Spend as much money as your budget can afford.

The actual rod length or brand will not be much of a factor in whether or not you catch fish fishing from a float tube. Haven't we all caught fish with the leader hanging in the water while we were fiddling with opening a fly box? The difference in rod length will be noticed in the ease of casting from your tube. A longer nine- to 10-foot rod lifts the line off the water easily enabling you to cast with less effort from your low position on the water. Roll casting from a float tube becomes a snap with a 10-foot rod. It seems that you can cast farther with the longer rod, too. We have learned that if you are going to fish day in and day out a longer rod makes casting a more enjoyable experience. However if you have a 7 or 8 foot fly rod and don't plan on doing much casting anyway, why let rod length stop you from float tube fishing? I'm sure you know that you can even take a spinning or bait rod out in the tube with you if that is your pleasure. The important message here is to buy a rod so you can get your gear together and start catching fish!

When you begin your search for a reel you'll feel like a kid in a candy store. There are many reels available with a few of them reasonably priced. They are all shiny and beautiful. You will need to buy a reel to match the rod you just acquired. You will not want to buy a saltwater reel to put on your trout rod. When I purchased my first reel money was an issue. The grocery money couldn't stand another hit that month. A conscientious salesperson tried his best to steer me in the right direction but I felt financially compelled to stick close to my budget. I purchased a huge "chunkmeister" reel that was on special. I can't remember if the word marlin was in the advertisement but I am sure it could hold a double without any difficulty. It definitely worked in lakes but by the end of the fishing day my arm was ready for a visit to the city morgue. I suffered in silence praying the reel would hurry up and break. It never gave up. As soon as I could afford the reel that I coveted

I gladly loaned "chunkmeister" to a friend who couldn't afford to buy a reel. He has had the reel for two years and I will never ask for it to be returned!

If you are unsure which reel will fit your rod, take your rod into the store and try the feel of different reels on your rod. Most rod manufactures have reel recommendations for specific rods. If the salesperson at the store is a qualified fly fisherman he or she will be a helpful mentor in setting up your rod with the exact reel you need. If you find a salesperson who knows nothing about fly fishing we advise you to run to the nearest exit.

Jim and I use different reels. They both happen to have drag adjustments on them. This is not a necessary feature. Your finger pressing against the line and rod can act as the drag, performing perfect line control as you play the fish.

There are many fly lines on the shelf in your favorite sporting goods store. There seems to be a line for every occasion (like a card shop) and the choices can be overwhelming. You can catch fish in any lake using a slow, intermediate or fast sinking lines along with a floating line. The full sinking line we use with most frequency is probably our intermediate uniform sinking line for water 10 to 20 feet deep. We also carry a fast uniform, full sinking line to get us down quickly beyond 25 feet. We do not use this line frequently but when needed you will be glad you have it. It is excellent for fishing minnow patterns in a deep lake. I also have and use a fast sink tip line. It is easy to cast and gets to the bottom quickly. We suggest you buy a floating line to go with the one or two sinking lines. You can always invest in different lines later on as your fishing career and experience progress. Extra spools of line don't take up much space in your float tube pockets.

When buying line make sure it matches your rod and reel. If you are a novice at fly fishing we suggest that you purchase all your gear at once. If you should receive a rod, reel or line as a gift be sure to take whatever you have to the store with you. It will save you time and energy and the store clerk's patience. Each rod is weighted to accept a certain weight of line. If your rod is a 5 weight the line you buy should be a 5 or 6 weight line in order to fit the rod. The line size should only go up one size higher than the number on your rod. The clerk will need to ask you a lot of questions and most of the answers will be right in front of him in the form of your equipment. After your explanation of how you will be fishing from a float tube in lakes, catching up to eight-pound trout, the salesperson will know exactly what type of line will be easiest for you to cast. He will probably suggest a weight forward, tapered line for your spool.

There is a balance test you can perform to see if your rod, reel and line are set up properly. Take the reel fully loaded with line and attach it to the rod. Place the rod across the place where your thumb would be if you were holding your rod for casting. With the rod lying across the underside of your thumb it should balance level. If it doesn't balance the rod will never be able to cast as it could have with the proper set up. Spend time and money wisely now and you will have fewer rod, reel or line regrets later on.

Retrieves and Twitches

*B*efore beginning any retrieve, shake or cast some line into the water. You will need to take your rod hand and place the line coming down from the last eye of the rod under the crook of your middle or index finger holding the rod. Now reach up to the line about five inches below your crooked finger, grasping the line above the reel with your free hand and pull the line toward your chest or stomach. Be sure to let the line slide past the index or middle finger. If you press tightly you won't be able to strip line in. Holding your finger pressed against the line and rod will act as a drag for playing a fish.

If you are in the water, practice pulling short retrieves of three to six inches of line at a time allowing the line to fall onto the float tube apron. Pull six to 12 inches of line. To set the hook lift your rod arm up high as though you were carrying a torch and pull one to three feet of line. (This is the correct height for pulling line in as fast as you can after you have hooked a fish and he is swimming at you as fast as he can.) Drop your rod arm and practice pulling long slow pulls as well as short quick pulls. This is how you retrieve your line from the water and is the basic strip posture for almost all retrieves.

Be creative and try a different sequence of pulls, perhaps two short and three longs. Experiment with different retrieves on a day the fish seem sluggish, when you aren't getting strikes. You will use the longer and faster retrieve to imitate a minnow swimming in the water. After a few fast strips allow your imitation minnow to pause as though he is looking for food or injured and begin the retrieve again. You will retrieve in short strips, quickly or slowly with long strips depending on the type of minnow or nymph you are attempting to imitate.

To use a Woolly Bugger or large nymph let out the desired amount of line and wait for it to sink close to or on the bottom of the lake. You will need to make anywhere from three to six pulls of line in increments of six to 12 inches. The pulls will be longer since you are attempting to imitate an insect that is larger and has the capability of moving fast when it wants to. Begin trolling the fly along the bottom of the lake slowly, stopping to let the fly settle. Now give the line three to four pulls. Release the line, letting the fly drop and settle to the bottom of the lake. Wait a few seconds before repeating this retrieve.

The next retrieve we will describe is the *hand twist retrieve*. One of the functions of this retrieve is to enable you to slowly crawl the fly along the bottom of the lake. This action will attract the fish as the fly kicks up a little mud just as a real dragonfly might do burrowing or swimming around the lake bottom. With this retrieve you may also bring the fly up to the surface at a steady controlled speed. Slow, medium or fast you will find this retrieve effective as well as relaxing. Practice until you get the hang of it and develop a good smooth rhythm. As you perform the retrieve you will basically be gathering line into your line hand and then either keeping it in your hand or letting it fall onto the apron of the float tube. This retrieve is also especially useful if you are bank fishing and want to keep your line off the ground or away from bushes.

Here is how we accomplish the retrieve: you already know how to place your line between your index finger and the rod to control drag. Next we would like you to apply light pressure to the line so you can gather the line into your retrieving hand. If you are right handed your left hand will be slightly extended in the handshake position. Pinch the free line hanging below your rod hand between your left thumb and index finger. Let the line between the pinched fingers drape over the back of your index finger and lie on the palm side of the three outstretched straight fingers. Close the three straight fingers over the line in the palm of your hand, the straight fingers being the middle finger, ring finger and small finger. From the handshake position rotate your hand to the right until your closed palm is facing the ground while simultaneously reaching up for the line with your middle finger, ring and small finger, in that order. This is a very quick motion as these fingers grab line pulling it into the palm of the hand. As the line is gathered you turn your hand back up to the handshake position and quickly pinch a new two to three inches of line and repeat the retrieve. Practice the retrieve. It only sounds complicated. Looking at the pictures on page 16 you will see how easy this retrieve is.

A question that we are often asked is, "What kind of a retrieve or strip do you use when there is a Woolly Bugger as an end fly and a smaller nymph being used as a dropper fly?" (Droppers are covered in the Droppers and Knots chapter.) If we don't know the lake and are in our searching mode we will probably fish the Woolly Bugger first. It doesn't matter which fly is fished first as long as you use a retrieve to simulate natural movements of the types of flies you have attached to your line. By adding smaller dropper flies we are trying to quickly increase our knowledge of what the fish are eating in an unknown lake. For example, at Round Lake during the *Callibaetis* hatch we don't tie on a weighted Woolly Bugger unless we are fishing unweighted *Callibaetis* nymphs and need something heavy to get the nymphs into the weeds. We fish the *Callibaetis* nymph as our primary fly.

As soon as we gain an understanding of any lake concerning the flies that work, we fish specific flies at specific times. Until you possess that knowledge you will have to try a variety of retrieves and flies. Three different flies might mean three different retrieves or three small nymphs might be fished with exactly the same retrieve.

Our basic small nymph retrieve is two to six quick, two- to three-

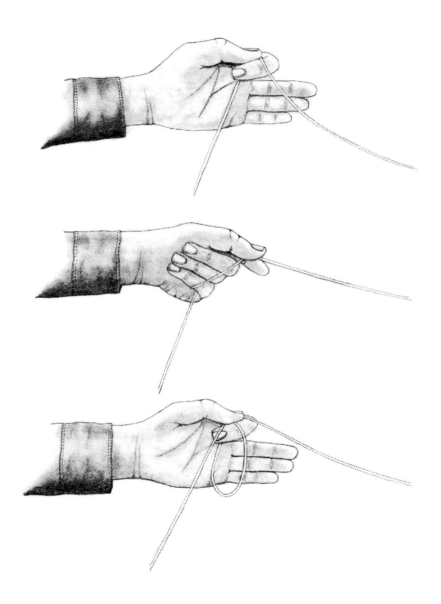

inch pulls. We then allow the fly to be still for about five seconds before repeating the retrieve. Sometimes we bring the small nymphs straight up from the bottom of the lake using the hand twist retrieve.

On some occasions you may need to vary the retrieve with changing water or weather conditions. The time of year, rise or fall in water temperature or even the speed at which you troll can dictate a change in retrieves. We have fished in conditions where the fish will only take the nymph after we have given it six to 15, two to three inch pulls. When we are having hot summer weather the fish will not take the small nymph if we barely troll at all. Using this knowledge you should be able to come up with a working combination of retrieves on any given summer day. The exception to the small nymph retrieve will be the way in which you retrieve the *Callibaetis*. We have hooked many fish moving the *Callibaetis* nymph slowly through the water using 10- to 15-inch slow pulls.

A question that may cross your mind is, "Why put the larger fly on the bottom of our leader?" Well, theory has it that if you are bringing your flies up from any depth perhaps the fish see the large bottom nymph you are retrieving chasing the smaller insects tied to your line. The opinion of some people is that this looks very natural to a fish in the water. Another logical reason might be that it is easier to cast line with the largest fly at the end of the line and the flies will line up better beneath the surface of the water.

The line twitch is not a retrieve since you do not bring any line onto the apron of your float tube. To begin the line twitch let out the amount of line you are going to fish with by either casting or backing away from the fly. Pull off a foot or two of extra line and drop it onto your apron. Your left hand is free to hold the loose line directly off the reel if you are right-handed. Begin by picking up the line from your lap with the left hand allowing the line to lie across the palm of your left hand. With your thumb keeping tension on the line pinched between the thumb and middle finger free movement of the first finger (index finger) of your left hand is allowed for twitching the line. The index finger does all of the twitching. You simply twitch the finger against the stretched line. The manner in which you hold the line will be the same for sinking line as well as for floating line.

To practice, place the fly in the water at the depth you wish to fish and using any retrieve pull in a foot or two of line and then pause. After the pause twitch the line a few times and then go back to the retrieve or simply use twitching to attract a fish. The twitch imparts action to any stationary fly but can also be used when trolling. Many times the fish will hit the fly just after the fly has been twitched. Other than fly selection the most important part of fly fishing is the retrieve or the action you impart to the fly, making the imitation appear to be alive.

Droppers and Knots

Droppers will enable you to fish more than one fly at a time. They can be added to your leader by tying the dropper line and leader or tippet together with a blood knot or surgeon's knot. The tippet material is used as a continuation of your leader. A surgeon's knot does look a little tacky, but it works. By leaving the loose end of the knot three or four inches long you will have enough length to tie a small fly onto the end of the short leader. If you leave the dropper leaders too long, they will fold back on your line when you cast creating tangles.

If you are a novice at casting start out by casting one main fly. After you are more skillful, add one dropper. It is easy for anyone to become frustrated untangling knots from droppers. If your skill level is such that three flies at one time pose no problems for you to cast, then go for it. If you are planning to fish without casting by all means tie on three droppers if the regulations allow it.

It is important to remind you to check the regulations at each lake for the legalities of fishing dropper flies. At some lakes regulations allow you to fish two or three droppers or as many as you can cast, while other places may allow none. The knots we use are the **blood knot**, **nail knot**, **surgeon's knot**, **clinch knot** and **Stren knot.**

Blood Knot: When tying the blood knot the recommendation is not to change line diameter by more than two pounds at a time. It is more practical to use a surgeon's knot when jumping in large increments from smaller to larger diameter.

Blood Knot

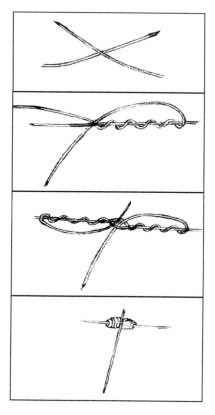

When tying a blood knot, start by crossing the end of the leader and the next size lighter piece of leader or tippet material.

Now wrap the heavier leader around the lighter tippet (four or five wraps). Then fold the end back and place it between leader and tippet, to form a Y.

Next wrap tippet around heavier leader four or five times and fold end back, sticking end through same hole at the Y. Both ends are through the same hole, facing opposite directions.

Holding both ends in place, wet the leader and tippet with saliva and pull leader and tippet apart until they form a tight knot.

Cut off one of the two pieces of leader if you are going to use the knot for a dropper line instead of a connecting knot. For a connecting knot you will trim both ends. If you want to fish the lighter tippet as a dropper for a smaller fly cut off the heavier leader leaving a stub of one-eighth inch at the knot.

Nail Knot

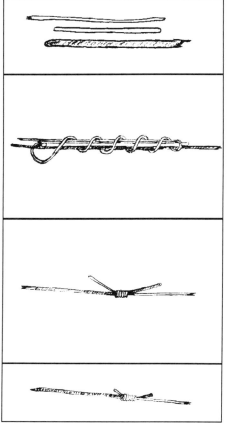

Place eight inches of leader facing in the opposite direction on the opposite side of the straw.

Holding the fly line, straw and leader together, fold the end of the leader back even with the straw. Wrap end of leader back across fly line, straw and leader, with at least six wraps. Fold the end of leader back and slide it into the straw, letting the end of the leader stick out of straw.

Holding leader wraps in place across leader, straw and fly line, pull the straw out. While holding everything tight between thumb and forefinger, slowly pull on leader until it is tight. Now you can release fly line. Pull main leader and stub of leader in opposite directions pulling the knot tight.

Finish by cutting off end of the leader and the end of fly line.

Nail Knot: The nail knot is used to attach the backing that goes directly onto the reel to your fly line or to attach the heavy butt leader to the fly line. We have found that a straw works better than a nail. Begin the knot by placing the end of the fly line along a two-inch piece of straw.

To make a nail knot even more foolproof you can fold the end of fly line over the straw before making the wraps with the leader.

Surgeon's Knot

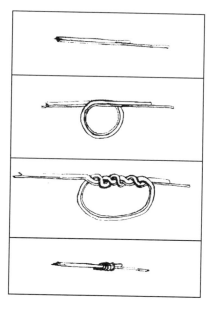

Start by overlapping the end of the leader and new tippet by five inches.

Make a loop in this doubled up area.

Now make three wraps with new tippet and the short five-inch piece of leader while threading them through the loop on each wrap.

Hold short ends while pulling the tippet and leader apart. Cut stubs short, leaving new one-eighth inch stubs

Surgeon's Knot: The surgeon's knot is used to join two far different diameters of leader. An example might be a four-pound tippet to a 10-pound leader. It can also be used in place of a blood knot by using one of the ends of leader from the knot for tying on a dropper fly.

Clinch Knot

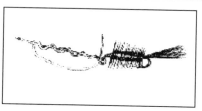

Clinch Knot: A knot used for attaching a size 10 or smaller fly to a leader. To tie the knot stick the end of the leader through the eye of the hook. You will want about three inches of leader to work with. Fold the end of the leader back upon itself and wrap the stub around the leader six times. Fold the stub back down sticking it between the hook eye and first wrap. Hold the stub and wet it with saliva, pulling on the leader to tighten knot.

Stren Knot

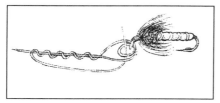

Stren Knot: Use this knot when you are tying on size 4 or larger flies. Begin by sticking the end of leader through the eye of the hook twice. Wrap stub around leader six times. Fold stub back, sticking the stub between hook eye and beneath the first two wraps around the hook.

Leaders

Leaders are used as a simple continuation of your fly line. To begin with the butt section of the leader, the end you tie onto your fly line, should be slightly smaller in diameter than the tip of your fly line.

The end piece of leader that you tie to the fly is called the tippet or tippet material. The length and strength of the tippet and leader will be determined by the size of the fish you are planning to catch or the size of the fly you are using. For example, perhaps you are fishing a small #20 dry fly to rising fish in shallow, crystal clear water. In order not to spook the fish you would need a long 12 foot leader that has a very light tip, such as a 2 to 4 pound test tippet.

The light leader will enable you to cast the small dry fly allowing it to land right side up with hardly a ripple on the water. At the other end of the scale perhaps you need to cast a large heavily weighted fly such as a #4 nymph. We can easily surmise that the long delicate leader that you used for a #20 dry fly won't have enough body strength to carry your heavy fly to the end of the cast. With the light leader your heavy fly will fold back onto your leader or fly line causing tangles and or knots. It is obvious that you need a shorter, stiffer leader to carry your heavy fly to the target.

To fish the heavier leader we would take the original 12 feet of light leader and cut it back to the heavier pound test we now need. If in a few hours a good hatch starts taking place on the surface of the water all you have to do is tie back on what you have cut off. If you have cut the leader back six feet to 8 to 10 pound test you will want to tie the new leader back on using a Blood Knot. It is recommended that you drop tippet size about two pounds at a time so you can get a nice taper to the leader and a good roll to the dry fly. To add the 6 to 7 feet of light leader back on, we would add two feet of eight pound test if we were working off of 10 pound test and then drop down to 1 1/2 pounds of six pound test. Next would follow about one foot of four pound test and the last tippet would be two feet of two pound test.

We suggest you buy a tippet or leader dispenser so you won't have to hunt through tube pockets looking for a specific size of tapered leader that you took off of your line last week or last month. It is nice to have store bought tapered leaders on hand if you can keep track of them after removing them from your line and storing them in your tube. Perhaps our organizational skills aren't what they should be but it seems much easier for us to make our own tapered leaders as we go.

When you prepare to purchase leader at the store you will see that most leaders are rated in X sizes as well as test pounds and diameter. Each manufacturer has different X ratings for the same pound test leaders. After we find a brand of leader that we have confidence in it is easier for us to purchase leader by the diameter rating thus eliminating the need for the X factor. We may use a heavier leader of .008 for large fish or a lighter leader of .004 for the lightweights or the easily spooked fish.

Another important thing to know about leader is how to attach it to your fly line. After purchasing an expensive tapered fly line you will not want to cut any of the fly line off. If you were to tie a tapered leader directly to the tapered fly line you would probably lose an inch or two off the end of your fly line every time you changed leaders. Before long your tapered fly line wouldn't have any taper left! Instead of tying your leader directly to the fly line tie on a couple of feet of butt material as we mentioned before. Try 20 pound test to see if it is slightly smaller in diameter than the fly line. Use the Blood Knot or make a loop in the end of both lines and lock the two loops together. This gives you the butt section of leader to work off of instead of the fly line. From this point you continue to taper the leader as we mentioned above or add your store bought tapered leader.

We often fish with three flies at a time so our leader starts out with the normal two feet of butt material then seven and a half feet of tapered leader down to 4 to 6 pound test. Now our leader is nine and a half feet long. To add the dropper lines cut back two feet of tippet and tie it back on with a Blood Knot to the leader leaving yourself a three inch dropper line. Add on two feet of new tippet leaving another three inch dropper. You will have a total of 11 1/2 feet of leader, two dropper lines and an end to tie the point fly onto. Always remember to test all of your knots by giving them a good tug. The "test" will save you lost flies as well as lost fish.

Depth Finders & Locating Fish

On our first visit to a lake we may not have a clue as to where the fish are hiding but we do have specific areas on any lake where we look for fish. First we check to see if there is an inlet or outlet at the lake. You may find fish foraging in these areas. The water temperature might even vary enough at the inlets to entice certain fish to hold in that particular temperature range.

When we see a lake that has good weed beds or even weeds along the shore we know that the fish are probably near. Some reservoirs lack good weed beds due to the variable water depths each summer and fall. Fish the outer edges of the weeds working your way in toward the middle of the bed unless you see a hatch taking place in one specific location. If there are good shore weeds there will be plenty of minnows hiding and insects hatching during the day. Hungry fish will be looking for prey attempting to hide amid the plants.

If you arrive at a lake and there appears to be nothing hatching, decide what color the bottom of the lake is and try to match the color with a Woolly Bugger. Caddis cases and nymphs are more often than not the color of the lake bottom. Search with dropper flies. Look for rock slides on the hills surrounding the lake. Brush hanging over the water can hold insects and make shade. On sunny days look for shadowed or shaded areas of the lake. Even a submerged log or rock will cast a shadow for fish to hide in on a bright day.

A best bet in locating fish will be a depth finder. You can actually strap one onto your float tube. It works well. I was made fun of when I came up with this idea but people laughing at me only serves to kindle my flame of inspiration. I decided that a float tuber should be able to have the same benefits as a boater when it comes to finding fish. After my brother-in-law Gale Sersain gave me some suggestions about how I might hook the depth finder to my tube I was off and running.

It didn't take but one fishing trip to quickly realize how blindly we had been fishing. We no longer waste hours of fishing time where there are no fish and no cover on the bottom of the lake. We do not need to take the depth finder with us every single time we go fishing. A person eventually learns where the fish are in the lakes during different seasons of the year.

We remember one lake where only two small fish showed up on the screen as we paddled back and forth across the lake. Within a few minutes we understood why there wasn't a soul fishing at this easy to reach lake. It didn't take us too long to figure out the lake had been fished out for the summer. At one lake we discovered our sinking line wasn't anywhere near the bottom of the lake. At another lake where we had been fishing dragging line along the bottom, we saw that most of the fish were holding at 10 feet. Keeping line at the right depth catches fish. Information like this saves you a lot of time, effort and energy.

Another—perhaps the main—use for the depth finder is to find out what the underwater terrain is like. We note drop-offs, ledges, gradual and radical depth changes, mounds and fingers of underwater land jutting out into a lake. We can see the weeds, logs and rocks on the bottom and follow any given depth around any lake that we care to. We get excited over the remarkable discoveries we have made about the lakes we fish, thanks to the depth finder.

One day at Haystack Reservoir we found a school of crappies in 20 feet of water. We went back and forth over the school catching the fish. At Wahtum Lake on Mt. Hood we were busy catching nine- to 12-inch brook trout when our tubes got too close to each other. Suddenly some monster fish started showing up on the screen. Talk about excitement! The excitement soon ebbed as we discovered that a friends' flipper was kicking right next to the transducer attached to my tube. We had a good laugh over that one. We are well aware that you cannot always see fish hiding on the bottom of the lake with a depth finder and most depth finders only cover a small area of water. We basically use the depth finder to gather important knowledge about the depth and underwater structure of a lake.

Here's how to attach a depth finder to your tube. First you will need go to the store and buy a small portable depth finder. Buy a webbed strap with a buckle attached that is long enough to go around your tube and around the base of the depth finder. Place the depth finder on your tube. Thread the strap under the screen and over the battery case. Tighten the strap. When you lift the screen the strap is not in the way. Mount the transducer on a 1 1/2 foot broomstick handle with a screw in the bottom of the transducer bracket. Screw the bracket into the side bottom of the handle. Hold the stick with the transducer attached to it against the outside of the strap on your tube. Mark where you will need to have Velcro® sewn onto the strap. You can staple Velcro® onto the stick where it will need match the Velcro® on the strap. Remove the strap from the depth finder and take the strap to a shoe repair shop. For a small fee the shoe repairman will sew the Velcro® you have purchased onto the strap. Bring the strap home and install the web strap with the Velcro® facing out. Strap the depth finder base back onto your tube. The stick may now be stuck to the strap.

I can't tell you exactly how many inches under the water my transducer is but I would guess that on my tube it is about 12 inches. There is absolutely no interference from my flippers. With a large piece of Velcro® on your stick you can adjust the depth of the transducer by a few inches. Remember that you will need to be moving in the water for the depth finder to work. My float tube has a strap around the circumference of the tube. In choppy water I tuck the end of the stick under the strap, ignoring the Velcro®. This keeps the stick stable when the wind starts bouncing you around. When hiking with your tube don't let the stick with the transducer on it bang on the ground as you walk. Put the stick with the attached transducer in a float tube pocket.

Jim and I fish from two different brands of float tubes. The float tube I use is a little larger than the one he uses. The depth finder works equally well on both tubes. Purchase a depth finder and don't go fishing without it!

Float Tubes

*F*or us a float tube is not only a device to get us away from the bank but an issue of comfort. Keep in mind that you will be spending many hours sitting in your tube. You must be comfortable or fishing will not be the pleasure it is meant to be. Float tubes can be purchased for a reasonable price. To us a reasonable price is a lot less money than you would pay for a boat!

After taking your tube to the lake and dressing appropriately for the occasion, slip into your fashionable flippers. Stepping through the holes in the tube intended for your legs, back into the water, pulling the tube up around your waist. Since you will be sitting down with your legs and flippers under you in this type of tube be sure to wade out into a couple of feet of water before attaching the crotch strap and sitting down. You will need this water depth to be able to kick your fins in water instead of mud. You may now sit back and relax.

For most people this is a comfortable tube. Jim loves this tube; I find it uncomfortable. It feels fine for the first few hours but as the fishing day wears on I start squirming. After making all of the manufacturer's suggested adjustments and not curing the problem I searched for a different tube. I found a tube that has an opening in the front with the tube in the shape of an U. The only drawback with this floating device is that it weighs more than Jim's tube. The extra weight makes a great difference if you have to hike uphill carrying the tube for any distance.

The V-shaped tube I use is designed more like an easy chair. To enter it put your fins on and holding onto the tube, back it into the water and sit down. Depending on how much you weigh you don't need more than 10 inches of water to launch. Your feet are not under your body but out in front of you, where your legs hang naturally as you propel yourself along.

Both tubes are well constructed with pockets and extra safety tubes. Mine has a little more room to attach a depth finder. Of the two a tube like mine will cost more.

Check the air pressure in your tube periodically. We check our tubes before every trip. We wouldn't want an unknown leak to develop overnight. Hot air expands and cold air contracts so don't leave an inflated tube in your car on a hot day with the windows rolled up. We also carry a foot pump in the car. For major trips we take an air compressor that is powered by the car battery. This is helpful to have if you need to let all the air out of a tube to make room for tents or gear. If you have never owned a tube and buy one, we suggest you buy an air gauge made for a float tube. The tire gauge made for large car tires does not measure five or six pounds of air pressure.

I was bursting with excitement when I finally purchased all of my own gear and couldn't wait to go to the lake alone. With my lack of experience I didn't have any idea of what six pounds of air would look and feel like in a float tube. The instructions said, "Beware of over inflating the tube." I did *beware* and under inflated the float tube. I hiked to a pretty little lake and donned all of my stylish new duds. I pulled my float tube up around my waist to wade backwards into the lake and unceremoniously sat down in my tube. I immediately had lake water running down my back and was afraid to paddle out any deeper. I was more than a little embarrassed and had no intention of drowning. I spent about an hour paddling around kicking up mud with my fins trying to cast out towards the deeper water. My beginning casting efforts were pitiful and I caught nothing. I acted as if everything was totally normal while I fished in the shallow, muddied, two to four feet of water.

When I decided that I had fished enough to let everyone think that I had planned to fish in this unusual manner I headed for an isolated bank and crawled out of my tube. I didn't dare take my waders off until I had hiked safely out of sight of the lake. After removing the waders I could wring lake water out of my clothes and was thrilled that I had an extra set of long johns stashed under the seat of my car. Fortunately I don't get discouraged easily. I learned from my experience and drove home with new determination. The next day I drove to the store and bought a float tube air gauge.

Did you know that Oregon law states that if you are out on the water in a floating device you need to have a life jacket in your possession? To save ourselves a hassle we both hook life jackets to our tubes. We should all be aware of safety as we practice our sport and it is definitely not a good idea to float tube alone. If you decide to go float tubing alone, hopefully there will be a boater or bank person around to offer assistance if you ever need any.

Jim tells the story about a fellow who was float tubing and got his line tangled around the end of his rod. Instead of pulling his rod apart he leaned forward trying to untangle the line. He reached out so far he tipped his tube over. He couldn't right the tube but somehow managed to swim out of it. This is the only horror story we have ever heard; we hope we never hear of another. We have come close to having leg cramps a time or two. One day we were out in the middle of a large lake when a big time wind came out of nowhere. It was a beautiful morning when we arrived at the lake. After we fished for a couple of hours the wind started blowing. We immediately began paddling against the wind heading toward shore. By the time our weary legs kicked us to shore the waves were breaking over the backs of our tubes. We finished our fishing day in a protected cove near the shore catching fish like crazy. The storm seemed to have pushed all of the fish right to us. We don't intentionally do anything foolish out on the water. We have the greatest respect for Mother Nature. She is not always good natured and forgiving like us!

Float Tube Pockets

*E*ven though this could be personal information we are going to list some of the items you will find in our float tube pockets. Fingerless gloves, a warm hat that will cover your ears as well as your head, a short rain jacket, nail clippers on a small diameter rope that you can hang around your neck. The clippers are cheaper than replacing teeth! A very small file for sharpening hooks, fly floatant to keep dry flies from sinking, a miniature scale to weigh a huge fish before you release him. A scale is better than lies! A plastic zip lock bag for collecting insects you might want to take home for closer observation, magnifying glass, a small pair of four-inch needle nose pliers for bending down barbs and removing hooks from fish. A stringer or fish bag (a fish bag can keep a can of pop cool), extra spools of line for your reel and extra leader ranging from two to eight pound test. Polarized fishing glasses are a necessity. A large man's handkerchief has a variety of uses: prior to blowing your nose and cleaning fish slime off your hands you can tail a large fish, use it to cover your face bandit style in case there are bugs annoying you or place it over your head like a scarf for emergency ear warmth. A water thermometer, insect repellent, Band-Aids, a small sharp knife, gum, licorice, canned juice or pop and, of course, lots of flies. We carry many flies; we only suggest you start out with the few we have talked about because they will give you a "head start" in the lakes. You will probably find many other flies that will also work for you. Part of the fun is to experiment on your own, learning and enjoying even more success.

When we begin a day trip we assume that we are going to one specific lake but we have found that we should carry flies for many lakes, because we can change our minds in a minute. All it takes for us to change our minds is for the other person to say, "I've got a good feeling about another lake today." As quick as a wink we are turning, heading in a new direction filled with a new spirit of adventure.

Waders, Shoes & Fins

It was a gorgeous hot summer day at the lake and I knew the temperature would creep up to a near boil as the day progressed. I waded out into the water and sat down in my tube wearing a shirt, shorts, stream boots and flippers. My family didn't hesitate to let me know that I looked comical but I did not care to spend another day with sweat running down the inside of my waders. As I kicked my feet in search of deeper water the weeds started brushing against and clinging to my bare legs. I thought leeches and starving fish were attacking my legs. It was awful! It makes me shiver just to think about it. I'll take a little sweat any day. By the way when float tubing on a hot summer day, after you sit down in your tube roll down your wader tops; you will be a lot cooler!

Most of the waders we see in Oregon are either latex rubber or neoprene. There are some manufacturers making waders out of a waterproof, lightweight coated cloth fabric which looks a whole lot cooler for summer wear. Jim likes a latex rubber wader and I wear a neoprene wader. They both can be bought in different millimeters of thickness. We have heard stories about waders not being sealed properly at factories prior to shipping. Even though the waders you buy are brand new we suggest you test them out for leaks in the bathtub before the first trip. This could save you a cold, wet body.

We have both been fortunate in our choices. I have worn my neoprenes without a leak for three years. Jim wears his latex waders to the river on occasion and has poked holes in them with berry bushes. His are easy to repair. He buys an inner tube patching kit and starts plugging up the holes. The neoprene patch goo that I use needs to cure for several hours before you can jump back into the water. Jim's latex waders actually stretch better to accept more clothing under them in the colder float tube months. Neoprene waders if thicker, can essentially be warmer to begin with.

For shoes we have chosen to wear a stream wading boot over our waders. You must buy the shoes a little larger than normal so they will accept the foot of your wader and a pair or two of wool socks. In order to get a good fit take your waders to the store with you. Put the foot portion of your waders on your feet with the socks you will want to wear and then try boots on. Instead of buying a stream boot you can choose a neoprene bootie. The bootie or sock pulls over the foot of your waders. Having tried both we have decided we prefer the stream boots. You wouldn't want to walk very far in the bootie as it does not offer much protection for your waders. The bootie fits snugly so it will stay on your foot in the water. This can make it difficult for you to pull it over the foot of your waders if you add a couple of pairs of socks to your feet.

In cold water conditions you will not be able to get your stream boots on over your waders when you add extra socks for warmth. This is when we set our boots aside. Jim puts thick wool felt boot inserts on over his feet, under his waders. I wear thickly padded slipper socks to give my feet the warmth they need. After you dress your feet and body for the cold, pull up the waders. It takes a little effort. Take a pair of old wool socks and cut straight down the tops six or eight inches so you can have enough room to pull them over the feet of your waders. They will protect your waders a little as you strap the fins right onto your feet. In order to get the fins to fit tightly on your foot without shoes on, step on the toe of one fin while you set your heel back as far as it will go and then tighten your fins onto your foot. Repeat for the other foot and the fins will stay on your feet.

When you shop for fins look for a flexible fin that's not too long. Long fins can wear your legs out although you can set speed records wearing them. You might also look for grommets at the eyes where the strings lace through the openings. The grommets keep the eyes from tearing out. We prefer front loading fins as they are very easy to slip your foot into and tighten up quickly with just a pull of the strings. The only fin hazard we have experienced was losing a fin to the Mud God and breaking a string. I will mention that it is about impossible to reach your own fin to tighten it when you are in a float tube unless you are a contortionist. It is a lot safer to ask a companion for assistance.

Rainwear & Cold Water Gear

A short wader rain jacket is an essential piece of equipment. Make sure it is waterproof not water resistant. There is a big difference when you are in the middle of a rain storm. The jacket is designed to be used with waders and it is lightweight and compact. Always keep it in the back pouch of your tube as it can also double as a windbreaker.

Speaking of rain jackets, there is a great story I like to tell about Jim taking me to Round Lake for my first lake fly fishing adventure. After getting a special dispensation from my husband to go to a lake with a strange man at 4:00 p.m. and not come home until after dark I wasn't about to back out of the trip because it was raining. Upon arriving at the lake the rain had turned into a downpour. Wearing borrowed things except for my own large full length fishing raincoat that leaked at the collar and shoulder seams, I prepared to enter the water. Noting that the raincoat was going to be in the way I asked Jim what I should do with it. He said, "I guess you can tuck it in." I obediently began stuffing all of the wet raincoat into my waders. I felt and looked as if I had been vacuum sealed with bulging tumors. I could hardly move. I got into the float tube and started fishing. I caught fish and was having the time of my life. I couldn't believe that I didn't know how to fly fish and could still catch brown trout. I was so thrilled with each fish tugging on my line I could almost forget the rain.

During this time I kept feeling water dripping and running inside my waders. I couldn't help wondering if I had a personal problem; maybe my skin had sprung leaks. Soon my teeth started chattering and my rod hand was doing a retrieve no man or fish has ever seen before. Not being a person to complain I clenched my teeth to keep them quiet and kept fishing by stabilizing my rod with both hands against my body. When the fishing action subsided and Jim said it was time to leave, I was very happy to get out of my tube. It was almost dark by the time I got all of the borrowed gear off and there was not one dry spot on my clothes. It was still raining! Jim cranked the heater up in his car and I dried out by the time I got home. I entered my house bubbling over with the joy of catching fish and I could hardly wait to go on the next fishing trip with Jim.

Believe it or not, all of our fishing is not done in the rain and cold. In early spring and late fall, the water can be cool and we have found a few ways to keep warm through the trial and error method. We found that our feet always get cold first. I spent some cold cash on electric socks. The electric socks are like trying to keep a barn warm with a firefly. We stuffed chemical hand and foot warmers into our waders but the fire would go out after about 30 minutes due to lack of oxygen. Nothing worked! Then Jim found some thick felt boot inserts around his house and stuffed them down into the feet of his waders. They were an enormous success: his feet were warm. I searched my house and found a pair of quilted Deer Foam slippers with nylon on the outside and a thickly padded sole. Bingo! They slipped into my waders easily and I, too, had warm feet. As the water temperature drops we add polypropylene and wool socks to our feet; we no longer experience frozen toes.

The next great discovery my fishing partner made was a one-piece quilted snow suit worn under his waders. Another slick idea! I didn't own a suit like his but I did have ski bibs and they work just as well. I like to layer with wool blend underwear, a turtleneck shirt and then a thick quilted shirt on top. The turtleneck comes in handy when your chin gets cold. Jim wears the same type of gear.

Hats & Glasses

*I*f you are not a hat person, become one. Start out with any hat as long as it offers protection from the sun, rain and errant hooks. Beginner fly fishing folks should not expose too much neck and ear. Perhaps you will want to find the perfect fishing hat that makes a statement about you and your unique personality. I keep searching but I don't think there is a hat out there that could make the proper statement for me. Until you find *the* hat, find any hat that has a bill on it. The bill can be very functional by keeping sun and rain out of your face. In a rainstorm, leave your hat positioned on your head and pull your raincoat hood over it; the bill keeps the raincoat hood from covering your eyes. It is nice to be able to see where you are going.

Invest in some type of polarized sunglasses to use when you are fishing. You need to protect your eyes from the harmful rays of the sun, the reflection off the water and stray flies. The glasses will also be effective in helping you to see fish in the water. For older eyes they even make these glasses with a magnifying lens which enables you to see to tie on tiny flies.

Fishing Tips

*H*ere are a few tips that may prove beneficial to you and your friends on your next fishing trip:

1. Bend down the barbs on hooks. This will save wear and tear on the fish. If you accidentally hook yourself it will save you a lot of pain. You won't need to worry about barbless regulations.

2. When you begin casting with a fly rod, always wear eyeglasses and a hat for safety.

3. Before casting a fly, consider the wind direction. The wind will either hinder or help you cast. For safety, keep the wind to your back until you become adept at casting.

4. When sitting in your float tube stripping in sinking line make sure you strip the sinking line onto the apron of your tube. If the retrieved sinking line is in the water it will sink and can become entangled around your legs and flippers. This may necessitate the help of a fishing buddy. Avoid the problem.

5. Remember this tip when you are fishing a fly on or near the bot-

tom of a lake that supports weed growth: If you feel three or four bumps on your line and haven't caught a fish within a few minutes bring the line up and check for weeds on the line.

6. If you are using floating line and a dry fly and the leader sinks after you have put floatant on the fly, rub the fly floatant on the leader about six to 12 inches above the fly.

7. Clean your fly lines periodically, following the manufacturer's instructions. It will make the lines much easier to cast and they will cast farther. On either floating or sinking lines when using a weighted fly, if you have a strike and miss the fish after five minutes or less, check to see if you still have a fly on the end of your line. Do not continue to fish the same fly if you are not getting strikes. If you see fish on the depth finder or know that fish are in the area, change the fly after 15 minutes or change the depth and location of where you are fishing. Don't waste time. Offer the fish a variety of flies until you come across the fishes' favorite meal. They will strike if you offer them the right imitation.

8. We have discovered that in many lakes from July to September the fish hold in deeper water. We often find trout 10 to 20 feet under the surface of the water.

9. After purchasing a sinking line you might want to consider marking the line at five or 10 foot intervals with waterproof ink pens. Color about six inches of line. This makes it easy for you to go right back to the exact depth at which you were catching fish. If you forget to count the marks off when you let line out count them when you bring a fish in.

10. Using sinking line you will notice that the more line you let out the more difficult the hook set becomes. Tie a size 6 Woolly Bugger and a couple of dropper flies onto your sinking line. Release 30 to 35 feet of line and allow time for it all to sink. After it sinks it will be easier to set the hook if you make the line taut by kicking your fins, backing up and removing any slack. Now drop your rod tip into the water as you sit back comfortably in your tube gently paddling with your fins. If you feel a strike or see the line tighten lift the rod tip straight up out of the water three to six feet, setting the hook. This gives you a straighter line to the fish in the water. We have lost fewer fish using this hook setting method with sinking line.

11. On a strike squeeze the crooked index of your rod hand against the rod holding the line tight while you set the hook. Then release some of the pressure from the line so the fish can be played without being broken off. When releasing line into the water be prepared for a strike. It is not uncommon for the fish to strike at the fly as it sinks toward the bottom of the lake. Always allow time for sinking line to sink before beginning a retrieve. Read the instructions on your sinking line. Different types of sinking lines sink at different rates of speed.

12. We rarely use less than four pound test and when we are fishing deep with large nymphs or streamers we never use less than a six pound test tippet or leader. We learned our lessons the hard way.

13. If you get a tangle in your leader when fishing multiple flies it is a lot faster to remove all the flies before taking the knots out of your leader.

14. If you hook multiples of fish take the top fish off the fly first. Also be careful when removing a fish when there are flies above the fish. If you have a hold of the leader and the fish makes a last effort to escape we can almost guarantee you will get hooked.

Striking Fish

When you are fishing a floating line (with wet flies or nymphs) you need to watch the distance of line from the rod tip to the water. As you retrieve you will notice that due to water tension the distance from the rod tip to the water remains the same as long as you strip at the same speed. During a good hatch it appears to us that fish are sucking up nymphs moving right on to the next one in line. When the fish inhales the nymph the action causes the distance from the rod tip to the water to increase. If you see this distance increase by one inch, set the hook and hold on. When fishing nymphs in this manner if you wait to "feel" the strike you will miss most of the fish. In order for you to catch fish with nymphs on a floating line it is imperative for you to watch your line where it touches the water, just off the rod tip.

When you are fishing on or near the surface with either dry flies or lightly weighted nymphs and you see the fish actively feeding but if you can't seem to hook the fish try this method. Cast and wait a second for the fly to settle. After the fly settles, raise your rod arm up slowly about six inches. Now drop the rod tip back to level taking up the six inches of slack with your left hand each time. This works well because as you raise your rod and a fish takes the fly your arm is already in the beginning of the hook set motion. You might have a tendency to set the hook too hard the first couple of times but you will get the hang of this and catch fish. This method works well when you are fishing mayflies, caddis and chironomid emergers from a stationary position in your float tube in up to eight feet of water.

Strike indicators can play a major part in hooking and catching fish. You will find a variety of indicators at your local fishing store. They are very inexpensive and most of them simply pinch onto your line. You will want to purchase one with enough color so you can see it on the water. The time to put an indicator on your line is when you can't detect the fish taking your nymph. To place an indicator on your line attach it to the leader just high enough to keep your fly off the bottom of the lake. The depth at which you place the strike indicator is the most important factor in hooking fish with an indicator on your line. You want to place your flies where the most fish are feeding. When the indicator dips under the surface of the water, set the hook.

Jim tells this tale about strike indicators. He was fishing with two friends and the friends were fishing two feet under the surface of the water with indicators. Jim was fishing near the bottom at five feet with his indicator. He caught many more fish than his friends. Strike detectors can be very beneficial if you are having difficulty detecting a sneaky take and will keep you at the depth where you want to fish.

If you are a novice at fly fishing as soon as you hook a fish try to get your line onto the reel. The first reason is you want the rod to play the fish. Never grab the line with the line hand and hold the line away from the rod. Keep the line under the rod hand with the finger pressed against the rod. You will be more apt to break the fish off if you play the fish with just the line in the line hand. Allow the rod to hold the fish.

The second reason is when you take the hook from its mouth if the hook isn't barbless it will necessitate taking the fish from the water and putting it on your float tube apron. This is where trouble can begin. We have had many ugly tangles in our line when a fish starts flopping around in loose line on the apron of a float tube. Untangling line can cut into fishing time as well as not being good for the fish you want to release. If you use barbless hooks you can usually shake the hook from the fish's mouth when you bring it up to the side of your tube. This way the fish will stay in the water and you will never handle it. This is the best method! We do not use a net since we generally fish with six-pound test leader which enables us to land and release a fish promptly.

If you hook a fish and it starts running at you 90 miles an hour you may not have enough time to get it on the reel. Even if you have it on the reel, you probably cannot reel your small diameter fly reel fast enough to take in the line faster than the fish was coming at you. Here is the solution for keeping up with a fish that is running straight at you. With your rod hand, hold the rod up as high as you possibly can above your head. Pretend you are carrying a torch. With your free hand reach up to just above the reel and start stripping in line as fast as you can. Be sure to use long strips with the free hand and keep the line close to the rod with the middle finger of the rod hand. Holding the rod high allows you to pull longer strips of your line onto your float tube with that free hand. Your goal will be to not let the fish have *any* slack in the line. After the fish turns and swims away from you it is easy to get the loose line reeled onto the reel while the forefinger of your rod hand gently applies pressure against the rod and line, keeping the fish under control.

Trying to put the fish on the reel when it isn't running takes only a little coordination. If you can't get it on the reel don't try to control the fish with your left line hand pulled away from the rod. Use the rod as much as possible for fighting the fish since that is one of the functions of a rod. Until the fish is on your reel your finger over the line on your rod hand should always control the fish. You will have more success catching fish using these techniques.

Fishing an Unknown Lake

We have had good success teaching people how to catch fish from a float tube by showing them a few basic arm movements with the fly rod and allowing them to progress at their own speed. Many people only want to catch fish with nymphs; it is easy to assist them in reaching their goals. Armed with desire, proper stripping technique and a cooperative fish so they can feel the strike and know when to set the hook, many beginners catch plenty of fish. Most people feel that fly fishing is too difficult for them to participate in. We are attempting to remove that myth from many minds. After getting the line into the water in our easy fashion it's the choice of fly and the treatment of that fly that makes or breaks a fisherman. Your casting may not be a thing of beauty but if you can catch fish without the casting and are having fun, who cares? You are still fly fishing, aren't you?

When you go to any lake follow this procedure. As soon as you step out of your vehicle take a long hard look at the area. Look at the ground where you are going to enter the water. Do you see any large winged ants? Do you hear any frogs or do you see any tadpoles? Are there crawdads? Roll over a log or large stick that has been under the water and see what is crawling around on it. Are there dragonfly nymphs trying to hide in the cracks of the wood? Look in the shallow water for damselfly nymphs and other water insects. If the wind is blowing plan on tubing the same direction as the wind so you can check out what shucks and insects the wind has stacked up near the shore.

Are there any fish rising? If so, try to find what insect they are eating. Check the air to see if any insects are flying around. If you see insects that you aren't familiar with and you think that there are enough of them hatching so the fish could be eating them, plan on catching one so you can see exactly what it looks like. Take the insect home at the end of the day in order to check out what the pupa or nymph might look like in *The Complete Book of Western Hatches*. After you catch the insect, try to match its size and color with one of the flies you have. When the fish are rising and you don't see anything on the water look more closely for small black or gray midges or gnats.

Did you know that 90 percent of the fish do their feasting under the surface of the water? Even if you see fish rising you will probably catch many more fish if you tie on a nymph pattern. We have frequently found that the fish surface feeding were smaller than we would normally catch on our underwater nymphs. We are successful catching fish because we fish nymphs the majority of the time.

Now that you know some of the things to look for we will give you a plan for fishing an unfamiliar lake. Upon arrival view the water. Perhaps you see a little gray mayfly hopping on top of the water in its mating dance mode. Most people would put on a floating line, tie on a small gray dry fly and go for it.

First decide how deep the water is where the most bugs are hatching. After observing the water you decide that the majority of bugs are hatching in about two to three feet of water. You already have guessed that you will need a floating line, long leader and one slightly weighted nymph. If you have any concern over getting snagged put a strike indicator on your leader in order to fish the fly just above the bottom of the lake. If you were going to fish in five feet of water you could get away with using two lightly weighted nymphs. Now you are ready to catch the fish in this area of the lake. It is a usually a clear plan of attack if bugs are out and about.

What do you do if nothing is visibly hatching? If nothing is hatching it is time to make educated guesses. You know that you will be fishing under the surface of the water probably on or near the bottom of the lake unless you are going to try some streamer patterns or dry flies. We'll assume you will stick to nymph fishing. If the lake is 15 feet deep in the area you have decided to fish put on your sinking line. Tie on nymphs that blend with the color of the water or lake bottom. Search for fishy areas—submerged vegetation and debris, edges of weeds, outcroppings of rocks, points, inlets and outlets to the lake. Tie on a variety of sizes and shapes of flies and begin searching.

Okay, you have decided to go fishing on the bottom of the lake in 15 feet of water. The water looks greenish to you as does the bottom of the lake. Start by tying a size 4 Green Woolly Bugger onto the end of your leader. The next fly on the first dropper will be a size 8 to 10 damselfly nymph or a green soft hackle. For the third dropper tie on a scud or chironomid. Why? Because every lake we fish in seems to have chironomids or scuds in them. Try different colors of chironomids—red, black, green and copper. Let line out until it hits the bottom of the lake. Check the colored marks on your line; it will be easy to let out the right amount of line each time.

Fish the green Woolly Bugger first giving it three or four long slow pulls, and then let it re-settle on the bottom of the lake. Next try three to four quick two- to three-inch jerks. Eventually you may want to change to a brown Woolly Bugger and fish it is as a leech or crawdad. Fish all the flies using the appropriate retrieves. Don't forget to use a slow hand twist retrieve imitating a dragonfly nymph crawling along the bottom. Still no hits? Let the line settle to the bottom again and fish your smaller nymph. Start the nymph off slowly with a steady hand twist for a foot or two and then give it a couple of twitches, making it jump. Pause and start swimming the nymph slowly to the surface with a slow hand twist. Pause again. This may allow time for the chironomid to look quite tempting. A strike! The fish took the chironomid!

When you find the fly that is "hot" tie on two of them. A hot fly does not catch just one fish. If you happen to find that only one fish will take your fly change the two that haven't produced and keep trying different sizes and colors. Always search for the perfect pattern that will catch the most fish.

Insects

*N*either of us are entomologists so we decided that we would simply stick to the words *bugs* and *insects*. I never would have imagined myself wanting to examine or touch a bug but we don't always seem to know what our futures hold. Collect the live insects you are attempting to imitate with your flies and bring them home in a bag of water to observe how they swim. I have a fish tank where I can easily observe anything I bring home. You will probably change the way you fish nymphs once you see the insects in action. To observe is to learn and by observing you will become more adept at fishing imitations.

If you want to keep your strange catch alive for a while remove the chlorine from the water with drops you can buy at the pet store and add an air pump to the water. Occasionally I wind up with a small hatch in the house but the little nymphs are totally harmless. It is a task catching them though. It is fascinating watching a nymph rise up to the surface of the water and wiggle out of its shuck. Within a few seconds it will be spreading its wings trying to lift off the water to fly away. Bear in mind that a nymph such as a mayfly is small, sometimes a sixteenth of an inch long, and does not make large jumps or movements in the water. Many times the small flies will make two or three small efforts to rise from the bottom and then rest. On the other hand a large caddis nymph can make numerous large wiggling movements. Caddis in cases are fascinating to watch, too.

One day my grandsons brought me a fantastic gift of a mama crawdad from the river. She had a ton of eggs under her tail. Everyone in the family had fun watching the babies hatch and turn into proper crawdads. We looked in on mom one day and found that she had shed her old dress for a bright new red one. All of this joy and insight came from an old aquarium that was used to house expensive tropical fish that died like flies. Now we keep interesting free critters in the tank and don't even have to pay to heat the water. Start your own collection of knowledge so you can write your own book. In the meantime we recommend that you purchase *The Complete Book of Western Hatches* by Rick Hafele and Dave Hughes if you are interested in learning more about insects.

Best Lake Flies

While shopping in the local fly shops I have overheard many telephone inquiries as to what flies will catch fish in the surrounding lakes on Mt. Hood. Well friends, our favorite lake flies tied and fished with the applications we describe will not only work on Mt. Hood but on just about any lake with similar hatches. Gather up some feathers and thread and prepare to tie one on!

Callibaetis Nymph, Weighted

Hook: Mustad 3399, sizes 16-14
Thread: Brown
Tail and Body: Three strands black moose mane
Collar: Dark olive Antron dubbing
Lead Wire: 10 wraps of 0.15 wire

At one time or another we spend money on a fishing book or magazine and wind up tossing the object aside feeling we wasted our money. Fortunately we have short memories and always truck back to the store to buy another "hot" book or magazine. We are always searching for that one bit of information that will add instant success to our sport. If Jim had known that the fly pattern for the *Callibaetis* Nymph he found in a magazine was going to be a winner at catching fish, I guarantee he would have willingly paid a much higher price for the article!

This mayfly pattern imitates a small gray fly with see-through wings, which have a black front edge. It sports a long white forked tail and has white legs. These flies bob up and down just above the water in their flying attempts. Once you see them you will think they have been sipping 100-proof alcohol; you'll know it's time to tie on a *Callibaetis* Nymph.

When fishing the *Callibaetis* Nymph we have been most successful catching fish on a floating line. Adjust the leader length for the water depth. The guide we use in fishing these nymphs is as follows: in water depths of one to three feet tie on one nymph; in water three to five feet deep tie on two nymphs; and in depths of over five feet you can use three nymphs (if the regulations allow three flies). When the fish aren't feeding near the surface of the water your success with this fly will depend on getting the fly close to the bottom weeds and then using a long, slow, steady retrieve. Use slow pulls of about 12 to 15 inches and pause for five to 10 seconds before starting another pull. Keep an eye on the spot where line and water meet. If there is any movement, set the hook. The fish have a tendency to sip this fly.

Cate's Turkey, Weighted

Hook: Mustad 9672, sizes 12-8
Thread: Brown
Tail: Dyed mallard flank, woodduck brown
Rib: Small diameter gold tinsel
Abdomen: Natural pheasant tail barbs
Thorax: Peacock herl
Legs: Dyed mallard flank, woodduck brown

*E*veryone should have a Cate's Turkey. In sizes 8-10 it may represent a caddis emerger. It represents emerging mayfly nymphs in the smaller sizes. The smaller versions of this fly work well when used as dropper flies.

You can use a slow hand twist retrieve or three to eight short, quick strips of six to eight inches each. Cate's Turkey also attracts fish when we use 10 to 15 quick, short strips. This fly produces well on both floating and sinking lines.

Carey Special, Weighted

Hook: Mustad 9672, sizes 12-8
Thread: Black
Body: Olive chenille or peacock herl
Hackle: Ringneck pheasant rump, long enough to reach a quarter-inch past the bend of hook

This is one of my favorite flies. It seems to be hard for fish to resist. The splayed pheasant rump feathers display plenty of action in the water to attract the fish.

To some fish the size of a fly is a major factor in whether or not the fly is accepted. Change sizes if you are not getting strikes. One hook size can be the difference between a many fish day and a fishless day. We generally fish the fly presenting it as a damselfly or dragonfly nymph. Begin fishing with the fly near or on the bottom of the lake near weed beds or shore. Retrieve the line with four to five long, slow pulls. Rest the fly for five seconds and make four to five quick six-inch pulls. This imitates the dragonfly crawling slowly along the lake bottom and then racing quickly for cover. This fly can also imitate a caddis dragging its case along the bottom of the lake.

Fish the Carey Special on a sinking line in deeper water and a floating line in the shallows. Try tying an unweighted or lightly weighted version of this fly and fish it on or near the top of the water in the fall. In the autumn strip the line in three or four six- to 12-inch strips and then allow the fly to be quiet on or near the water surface for about 10 seconds before stripping or wiggling it again. We have had some interesting results with this technique especially in the shallow water at Round Lake.

Chironomid

Hook: Mustad 94840, sizes 16-10
Thread: Black
Rib: Smallest diameter silver tinsel
Body: Black, olive, tan, brown or red floss or Swannundaze
Head: A dubbing to match body
Collar: Four wraps white ostrich herl

We seem to find chironomids in every lake we fish. They may not be as plentiful when the weather turns cooler but we always seem to see a few hatching. In most lakes after the water warms up the insects start hatching in the mornings and continue hatching throughout the day tapering off around three or four in the afternoon. Chironomids hatch in the deeper sections of the lake as well as the shallows. The emergers seem to draw the most attention from the fish.

Using a long leader, we tie one fly on each dropper line and cast allowing the flies time to sink. Then we employ a steady, slow hand twist retrieve. After pulling in three to five feet of line pause for about five seconds and give the line two or three finger twitches. Pause another five seconds and start the pull again. You may fish this fly on floating, fast or intermediate sinking lines depending on the depth of the water. Fishing the chironomid slowly in deep water enables us to catch fish in the middle of a hot summer day when nothing seems to be hatching.

When fishing deep water do not necessarily retrieve all of the line. You want the right amount of line out at the right depth to catch the fish. After you retrieve most of your line shake or wag the rod tip slowly from side to side, releasing the line. Backing away while kicking your fins allows the line to slither down to the depth where it needs to be. This way you can keep the fly at the fish-holding depth for a longer period of time. When this fly is fished in deep water the fish usually hit it so hard you don't need to guess about whether you have had a strike.

When you are fishing chironomids near the surface of the water a strike indicator can be a helpful fishing tool for you to use.

Damselfly Nymph

Hook: Mustad 9672, size 12
Thread: Olive
Tail and body: Olive yarn
Thorax: Olive dubbing
Legs: Pick out dubbing
Rib: Gold, optional
Wingcase: Dyed olive pheasant tail

*W*hen tying the fly keep it very thin. Fish it weighted or unweighted. The Damselfly Nymph that Jim ties has gone through an evolution. We have had a great deal of success with this version. We find that it out fishes our old patterns three to one giving us a lot of confidence once we spot the real nymphs swimming in the water. Try this pattern at Gold Lake in the spring and early summer as well as at all of the other lakes.

Fish the fly on either floating or sinking lines. You may need to vary the retrieve depending on the time of year. We generally pull a few short quick strips of two to six inches and then allow the fly to sit quietly before repeating the retrieve. If the fish appear disinterested in the nymph adjust your retrieve. We have found a steady, medium hand twist retrieve will also work if you add occasional quick jerks. The real damselfly nymph puts a lot of wiggling motion into its small body. It can be found near the surface of the water or on the bottom of a lake. The retrieve is the key to catching fish on this fly and you may have to adjust the retrieve for a specific lake.

Deer Hair Caddis

Hook: Mustad 94840, sizes 16-10
Thread: Brown
Hackle: Dyed grizzly to match body
Body: Olive, tan, gray or black
Wing: Deer body hair

Elk Hair Caddis, Light

Hook: Mustad 94840, sizes 14-10
Thread: Tan
Hackle: Light ginger
Body: Light yellow or light tan dubbing
Wing: Elk hair rump

The caddisflies mentioned above are found to be effective in almost every lake we have ever been to. You might have to wait for a specific time of day but insects matching these patterns will probably eventually hatch. You need to carry several of these flies in different sizes. When the real caddisflies hatch they seem to hit the surface on the run. They are very active in their attempts to run and fly away. It appears to take them three or four attempts to escape the water's surface.

After tying the fly to your floating line treat your fly with floatant. Using 10 to 12 feet of leader you will be ready to cast. Once the fly hits the surface of the water slide it a foot or more, pause, count to 10 and slide it again. The fish may have to make several attempts to catch the imitation. This is an easy retrieve. You and the fish will have plenty of excitement with this fly.

Gold-Ribbed Hare's Ear

Hook: Mustad 3399, sizes 16-10
Thread: To match body
Tail: Dyed grizzly hackle to match
Rib: Flat gold tinsel
Body: Rabbit dubbed in tan, olive, gray, black or yellow
Wingcase: Dyed ringneck pheasant tail
Legs: Dyed grizzly hackle to match

As you tie the fly make the thorax thicker, tapering the body from the abdomen to the tail. Be sure to pick out longer hairs to imitate legs. You can fish the Gold-Ribbed Hare's Ear weighted or unweighted as a wet or dry fly. This fly can imitate mayflies, *Callibaetis* or caddis nymphs. Tie different colors and sizes to allow you to match what is hatching any time of the day.

If you are fishing the Gold-Ribbed Hare's Ear as an emerging fly (a *Callibaetis* nymph for example) let it sink and then bring it up to the surface in long, slow, even strips. Pull an arm's length (10 to 15 inches) at a time slowly. After five slow pulls, pause and continue the sequence again.

When casting to surface feeding fish using a floating line, cast directly into the rise ring trying not to allow the fly to sink. Control the fly by lifting the rod tip up slowly letting it drop slowly back down and repeating. You are attempting to bring the fly up in front of surface feeding or near surface feeding fish. If no strike occurs after a few attempts, cast to another rising fish. The normal retrieve for fishing this fly will be short quick jerks on the line.

Gray Hackle Peacock

Hook: Mustad 3399, sizes 16-10
Thread: Black
Tail: Red hackle fibers
Body: Peacock herl
Hackle: Grizzly

J im was fishing on a lake with a couple of friends when he started catching fish on an Olive Woolly Bugger using his intermediate sinking line. He was fishing with beginners who didn't own sinking lines, so he changed his line to match theirs in order to find a fly that would work for them. It took 45 minutes and about 10 fly changes for him to find what the fish would strike. He noted that there were no apparent hatches going on. Through trial and error he found the Gray Hackle Peacock was the only fly the fish would hit on a floating line.

After tying on the right fly his friends caught lots of bass.

We have found that bluegill, trout and crappie like this fly. Fish it on all types of lines—whatever the water depth dictates. Use a short, quick strip retrieve. Try two- to four-inch strips with six or seven pulls, pause and repeat.

Green Caddis Emerger

Hook: Mustad 9672, sizes 12-8
Thread: Brown
Rib: Heavy brown thread
Abdomen: Olive yarn
Wingcase: Natural pheasant tail
Legs: Natural pheasant tail extending back past bend of hook
Thorax: Tan dubbing

*T*he first time we noticed one of these bugs swimming around we thought it was the most peculiar looking insect we had ever seen. It was dark olive green on its back, light tan in the front and had legs longer than the body. The whole thing was about 1-1/4 inches long. This bug is a steady, smooth swimmer and seems to swim about one foot under the surface of the water.

It is always amazing to see what Jim ties after we find a bug. I couldn't believe he could capture the exact likeness of this insect. This lightly weighted fly usually gets strong takes. We have had good results fishing it a variety of ways. Try to fish it about one to four feet from the surface on floating line. The strip is medium speed in one-foot pulls. Pull in about four to six feet, pause and repeat. After retrieving three-quarters of your line let the line out and start over. We have also caught fish on this fly on our fast and intermediate sinking lines fishing deep water with long, slow retrieves.

Iron Blue Wingless

Hook: Mustad 3399, sizes 16-10
Thread: Red
Tail: Honey dun hackle fibers
Body: Rabbit dubbing, gray
Hackle: Hackle, honey dun

*T*his weighted fly imitates a type of nymph or ant. It catches fish for us on a consistent basis. When you can't pinpoint exactly what the fish are feeding on tie on the Iron Blue Wingless using it as a dropper fly. We often fish this fly in conjunction with a Soft Hackle as a main fly. Fish it on either floating or sinking lines depending on water depth. The retrieves will be three to eight quick, short strips of four to eight inches or a long slow pull of one to two feet. Try using the hand twist retrieve. The Iron Blue Wingless changed a fishless day into a productive day at Timothy Lake.

Midge, Black or Gray Herl

Hook: Mustad 94840, sizes 18-12
Thread: Black
Tail: Hackle fibers, to match body
Body: Black or gray ostrich herl

*W*hen the midge hatches it will spin wildly about on top of the water preparing to take off while other midges are buzzing around you. Midges usually have a lot of pals nearby.

This is one fly that is often better smaller. We fish the midge on a floating line as a dry fly. Before you begin to fish grease all but the last few inches of your light, long leader and place one midge on your line.

Cast the line and allow the fly to sit quietly on top of the water. If the fish are ignoring the fly wiggle it occasionally on top of the water. It will look like a struggling midge trying to escape the surface film.

It is indeed fun watching a fish take a dry fly such as a midge. You are going to be challenged to keep an eye on your imitation midge. It is easy to lose sight of the imitation around the living specimens on the water.

One day when I was fishing this fly I sat in my tube watching the wrong midge on the water for three minutes. When the one I had been watching was taken, I set the hook. I was really surprised when there was no fish on the end of my line.

Muddler Minnow

Hook: Mustad 9672, sizes 10-2
Thread: Brown
Tail: Section from turkey wing
Body: Gold tinsel wrapped over two-thirds hook shank
Underwing: Gray squirrel
Overwing: Paired sections of turkey wing, tied on edge.
Head: Spun deer body hair clipped to taper, forming collar of long hairs at rear of head.

*T*he Muddler Minnow is our second favorite fly. It was originally tied to imitate a sculpin or minnow and was meant to be fished as a bottom fly.

Fish the Muddler as a dry or wet fly. You may weight it and fish it in deep water or use a sinking line to take it down. On floating lines fish it just under the surface or on the surface of the water.

To retrieve the fly on floating line as the fly sits on the surface of the water, allow the fly to settle and strip in long, slow pulls. If this doesn't attract the fishes' attention alternate one long strip with two or three short, fast pulls. You can create a nice wake on top of the water with this fly to tease a fish into a vicious strike by trolling in your float tube. This fly is very productive fished in the evenings on almost any lake.

Pheasant Tail Nymph

Hook: Mustad 94840, sizes 16-6
Thread: Brown
Tail and Body: Pheasant tail
Legs: Pheasant tail
Wingcase: Pheasant tail
Rib: Gold, optional

This little fly can imitate many different insects. Small, the fish may take it for a chironomid; medium, a mayfly; and large, a caddis. It is an excellent searching fly. We have used this fly on days when we didn't know what the fish were taking and have caught many fish.

The retrieve will have to be performed for whatever type of insect you are going to imitate. You might crawl it along the lake bottom for a caddis or bring it up towards the surface of the water slowly for a chironomid. You will have to think about what insect you are trying to imitate before beginning any retrieve.

We have even tied gray legs on this fly and caught many large fish at Timothy Lake. Don't leave home without a Pheasant Tail Nymph because it works well in many of the lakes!

Rabbit Leech

Hook: Mustad 33960, sizes 8-2/0
Thread: Black
Tail and Body: One piece black rabbit fur

*I*n Oregon it is not illegal to fish for bass in warmwater lakes at night, but it is illegal to fish for trout at night in the same warmwater lakes. Always check the regulations for each lake you fish. The Rabbit Leech is a "must have" fly for catching bass at night. It also works very well in Washington lakes where it is legal to fish for trout at night.

When you are fishing for bass at night you will usually be fishing the surface of the water. Fish the Rabbit Leech near bank areas and retrieve it slowly or troll it in shallow water. If you aren't getting hits allow the Rabbit Leech to be still. Give it an occasional twitch before resuming your troll or retrieve. If you are trolling there will be no need to hand twist your line in at the same time.

Fish this fly on sinking or floating lines depending on the time of day and the depth at which you wish to make your presentation to the fish. You should use an eight-pound tippet or leader because the fish can attack the Rabbit Leech. You will find a fast hand twist retrieve creates a continuous, medium swimming action for the leech if you want to fish from a stationary position in your float tube.

Most leeches have the appearance of flattened worms and are primarily nocturnal. Colors can range from black to gray, brown, olive or cream. The size variation is from one inch to six inches long. As they swim their bodies undulate in a wave pattern. They can be found on the bottom of lakes or suspended vertically near the surface. This can be a killer fly.

Royal Bucktail Coachman

Hook: Mustad 33960, sizes 8-4
Thread: Black
Tail: Golden pheasant tippet
Rib: Small diameter silver tinsel
Body: One-eighth peacock herl, three-quarters red floss, and one-eighth peacock herl
Hackle: Coachman brown
Wing: The white underside of a whitetail deer tail or calf tail

*U*nder normal conditions in October and November fish this fly on a floating line as a streamer. In the fall the fish seem to strike the fly just under the surface of the water. The strip is very fast and the fish take the fly hard. We found an exception to this rule fishing in one of our lakes this summer.

The spring and early summer of 1993 was exceptionally wet and cold. The insects were not very cooperative in hatching so we decided to try the Bucktail Coachman at one of our lakes. After fishing it properly with no strikes we started talking to each other with the fly sitting still in the water as we barely trolled. We twitched the line a couple of times and continued to talk, giving the fly very little movement at all. Suddenly we had a fish! We continued to catch fish for two hours while fishing the Royal Bucktail Coachman with a couple of twitches and then doing nothing but letting it sit idle. It was a remarkable experience. We couldn't believe the fish wouldn't touch the fly if it was moving.

Scud

Hook: Mustad 3399, sizes 16-10
Thread: To match body color
Shellback: Dyed pheasant tail
Body: Rabbit dubbing, olive, black, gray, tan, orange or yellow
Cement: At least four coats of clear coat head cement on shellback for gloss

*F*ish this fly in shallow water on a floating line. Occasionally it takes fish in deep water on a sinking line. Scuds seem to appear everywhere in a lake, especially around any type of weeds, mossy rocks or submerged logs. You will need to use a quick, short jerk strip of one or two inches. After eight to 15 strips pause about five seconds and then repeat the retrieve. Sometimes the amount of short strips is critical to the take.

We have also caught fish on a soft orange scud. It is our opinion that the fish may hit this particular color thinking it is a freshwater shrimp. If you get the opportunity to catch scuds take some home from the lake, pop them in an aquarium and watch them swim. Some almost appear to be hopping under the water.

Scud, Special

Hook: Mustad 3399, sizes 16-10
Thread: Olive
Shellback: Pearl Krystal Flash, 15 strands
Body: Olive Antron dubbing, applied with a soft dubbing loop

*T*ry tying these flies in both light olive and dark olive. We also have a tan and orange in our arsenal. We use this fly as a secondary dropper fly. Be sure to keep the dropper flies at least 24 inches apart and above the larger fly tied at the bottom of your leader. If you are fishing weighted flies always put your largest, heaviest fly at the end of the leader. We have also used this same pattern to represent a beetle by changing the color to black. We often experiment with different colors to see what the fish will hit. Use the same retrieve as you use for the scud, a short one- or two-inch jerk retrieve.

Soft Hackle

Hook: Mustad 3399, sizes 16-10
Thread: To match body color
Rib: Gold tinsel
Body: Rabbit dubbing, tan, brown, olive, black, gray, or yellow
Hackle: To match body color

*W*hen you watch your Soft Hackle moving through the water it will have the appearance of being alive and breathing.

With different colors and hook sizes to choose from you will be able to catch fish with this fly even though you don't see any bugs hatching.

The knowledgeable fly fisherman has discovered that this fly imitates many types of underwater hatches. We often use the Soft Hackle as a searching fly. Try several of the different retrieves to fish this little fellow. The only retrieve that will not work is the minnow retrieve.

We begin our presentation of this fly by making it appear to breathe by working it in quick short strips and then pausing. If this doesn't wake the fish up use different methods of bringing line in until you find a retrieve that will work on the fish for that day and lake. Use this fly on floating or sinking lines.

Spruce Fly

Hook: Mustad 33960, size 8
Thread: Black
Tail: Peacock sword
Rib: Small flat silver tinsel
Body: Red floss, two-thirds hook length
Thorax: Peacock herl
Wing: White marabou; two strands of pearl Krystal Flash
Hackle: Badger hackle, three wraps

*T*he Spruce Fly is another good searching fly. The main retrieve is a swimming minnow imitation stripped fast for five or six long pulls, paused about five seconds and the strip repeated. In deeper water we fish this fly on intermediate or fast sinking lines. For shallow water use a floating line with about 12 feet of leader. Even though trout seem to have a strong preference for this fly in the fall we still catch fish on it regularly all summer.

Tied-Down Caddis

Hook: Mustad 94840, sizes 16-10
Thread: To match body color
Hackle: To match body color
Body: Yarn or floss, orange, yellow, gray, brown. black, olive or red
Wingcase: Dyed pheasant tail
Tail: Pheasant tail tips

*I*f we rated our flies on a scale from 1-10 this fly would be in the top five. The Tied-Down Caddis has proved to be one of our best flies. When fishing this pattern, remember that most caddis larvae live near weeds where they can find plenty of food to eat. We have observed many hatches in shallow water (10 feet or less). When fishing your fly as an imitation for caddis use a floating line. That's not to say you won't catch fish on this fly in deeper water using intermediate sinking line. Perhaps the fish take it for something other than a caddis in the deeper water.

Tinsel Fly

Hook: Mustad 9672, size 12 or Mustad 33960, size 4
Thread: To match body color
Body: Silver or gold tinsel, weighted with six wraps .035 lead wire or unweighted
Wings: Silver or gold Flashabou extending a half inch beyond the bend of the hook; tie Flashabou in at hook eye, let Flashabou extend a half inch beyond the eye then fold the Flashabou back one-third over body and tie down

*T*his is the fly that was inspired by the Flatfish. Fish it as you would a streamer or a minnow pattern. Unweighted we fish it on floating lines with 10 to 12 feet of leader so we can fish it on the surface of the water. Fish the weighted version under the surface. Retrieve it as you would a minnow pulling long, fast pulls until your arm wears out or all your line is in. Then it's time to cast again. Occasionally we stop the stripping in mid retrieve before the line is all in. Stopping the retrieve can work to entice a fish that has been chasing the minnow to hit it.

Your sinking line simply runs the fly deeper. If the fish are not hitting this fly near the surface, offer it to the fish that are suspended near the lake bottom. We fish silver in the bright sun and gold on a dull day.

Uncle Dudley

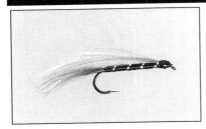

Hook: Mustad 33960, sizes 8-4
Thread: Black
Tail: Red hackle fibers
Rib: Small diameter silver tinsel
Body: Black floss
Wing: Two honey colored hackles
Legs: Red hackle fibers
Cheeks: Golden pheasant tippet

*U*ncle Dudley is another fly fished as a streamer fly. Fish it primarily on a floating line. It can be fished in the same manner as the Royal Bucktail Coachman. We have the most success with this fly in the fall.

Cast, allowing the fly to sink. Retrieve in fast, long pulls. We also use the rod tip to make the minnow change direction being careful to keep the slack out of the line with our retrieving hand. You can pause in the retrieve before beginning erratic swimming movements again. Think like a minnow: foraging, looking around then in a burst of speed heading off in a new direction.

Water Boatman

Hook: Mustad 94840, sizes 14-10
Back: Dyed pheasant tail
Legs: Dyed grizzly hackle to match color of body, palmered
Body: Yarn, yellow, orange, olive, black, brown, and tan
Cement: Four coats clear head cement on back of fly for gloss

*O*ne day we were paddling along in our float tubes at Haystack Reservoir and we kept hearing small splashes. Finally we saw a water boatman landing and taking off. It had taken us years to see one fly. If you want to see speed just watch this fellow swim—we guarantee he can pass you. Fish the Water Boatman on sinking or floating lines although you will possibly experience more success with it on a floating line. This is a fly to try when you do not know exactly what the fish are feeding on at any given time. For evening fishing try plopping down a larger size in very shallow water.

The water boatman comes to the surface for a bubble of oxygen that he holds between his hind legs. He uses the bubble to obtain oxygen since he does not have gills. The bubble covers part of his underside giving him a shiny appearance in the water. These insects swim on their backs making erratic, fast swimming movements. They search for food on the lake bottom and then have to surface quickly for oxygen.

After allowing time for this fly to sink use a retrieve pulling one-inch strips very fast, giving the line a sequence of 12 of them. Pause for three seconds and start again. Fish often take this bug hard probably because they are afraid the insect will get away from them.

White Marabou Minnow

Hook: Mustad 33960, sizes 8-4
Thread: Black
Body: Pearl mylar tubing
Wing: White marabou

*J*im and a friend had planned their first trip to Hosmer Lake. They fished for three days and hadn't experienced much success. They had witnessed a couple of men catching fish as fast as they cast their flies in the water. Jim could only make out the color at the end of their lines. These gentlemen had arrived at the lake in the early morning hours and had left their car lights on all day. When they were ready to leave their car would not start so Jim offered the services of his jumper cables. In return for the jump he begged a handful of their "good" flies. Since that time we have caught more than our share of fish from these white minnows.

The stripping method for the fly is simple: fast and faster, stripping in long, fast pulls. You may fish the minnow on either floating or sinking lines with the minnow being weighted or unweighted. The line you choose will depend on the depth of the lake and the level where fish are suspended or feeding.

Woolly Bugger

Hook: Mustad 94840 or Mustad 33960, size 12-4
Thread: To match color of the body
Tail: Marabou to match body
Hackle: To match body
Body: Chenille in black, brown, tan, red or olive

*I*f we could only fish with one fly this would be the one we would choose. Weighted or unweighted, in different colors and sizes it represents a multitude of different insects. A large size 4 brown might represent a crayfish if presented properly. Crawl the fly slowly then use quick strips have it escape along the bottom of the lake. The fish may think the large brown, red, black or cream Woolly Buggers are dragonfly nymphs or leeches undulating or crawling across the bottom or surface of a lake. A size 12 black, brown or olive might convince the fish it is a caddis case lying among the bottom weeds and debris of the lake. The smaller size 12 brown or olive green can represent a damselfly or small dragonfly nymph searching for prey or migrating toward the shoreline.

Large nymphs can move fast when they have to. We have observed them hiding in the weeds and then swimming off to search for food.

When frightened they propel their wiggling bodies back into the safety of the weeds. We have found that a large size (4) works well in late spring. As July approaches, at some lakes you will need to start using smaller Woolly Buggers. Fish to imitate dragonfly nymphs on the lake bottom, pulling them slowly along. Allow them to settle and then give the line a couple of quick six-inch strips, pause and repeat. Vary your presentation by pulling three to five quick six- to eight-inch strips and then allowing the line to sink back to the bottom.

Zonker Minnow

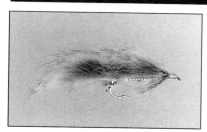

Hook: Mustad 33960, size 4
Thread: Black for head
Thread: Red, for tying down rabbit fur butt
Underbody: Zonker tape
Body: Pearl mylar tubing
Wing: Rabbit fur strip, olive or gray
Hackle: Grizzly

*T*his fly is an excellent fall trout fly. Fish it when the trout are trying to fatten up for winter by eating unsuspecting minnows. This is a great minnow imitation. We strip this fly long and fast on sinking or floating lines. We happen to catch more fish using the floating line and have had limited success with sinking lines. We pause occasionally to let the fly rest and then start the quick retrieve once again.

Zug Bug

Hook: Mustad 9672, sizes 12-8
Thread: Black
Tail: Peacock sword
Rib: Small diameter gold tinsel
Body: Peacock hurl, lightly weighted
Wing: Dyed mallard flank, woodduck brown
Legs: Coachman brown hackle

Weighted or unweighted, the Zug Bug imitates many underwater insects: dragonfly, snail, spider, caddis cases and nymphs, just to name a few. If you do not want to catch bluegills, don't use a size 10 or 12.

Fish the Zug Bug shallow or deep depending on the species of fish you want to catch. We usually catch trout on it in deeper water and pan fish in shallow areas. Trout take the size 8 to 10 hook quite readily in most lakes. In the summer we slowly troll with an intermediate sinking line, twitching the line occasionally. If you aren't getting hits you must try working it differently. Let the fly sit on the bottom quietly and then twitch or pull in long slow strips for two or three feet, allowing the line to free-fall back to the bottom.

In shallow water fish the fly on floating line with the regular 10 to 12 feet of leader. Retrieving flies is an art. The proper retrieve can be the difference between catching fish and just fishing. Practice and experiment until you find what motion causes a fish to strike. Once you discover the perfect retrieve for a specific lake and fly go home and write it down. You don't want to forget the perfect recipe for retrieving.

Lakes of Mount Hood

When we informed people that we were writing a fishing book one concern we heard repeatedly was "give us good directions to the lakes." We did! We hope that the directions as well as information on flies, fishing techniques and the maps of each lake will prove to be a valuable catching asset to you. These maps are not to scale.

Badger Lake

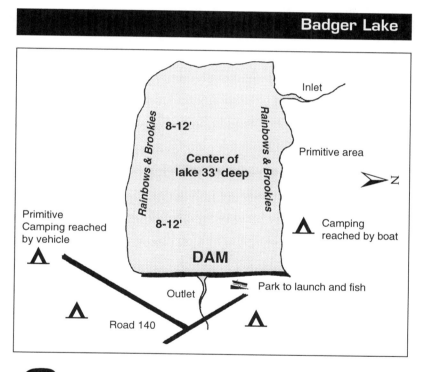

*O*ur first trip to this secluded 35-acre lake was on a very hot day in the middle of July. Arriving at the lake we launched our float tubes 50 feet from where we parked our vehicle. We saw plenty of fish on the fish locator and a few were good sized. The only other activity we saw on the water was a canoe and a bait and spinner fisherman rowing his boat around the lake. The gentleman who was fishing informed us he hadn't caught any fish in two days.

After we spent a couple of hours drowning our nymphs without a strike we noticed many fish beginning to rise near the banks. We quickly changed from sinking to floating lines and headed to the shaded side of the lake. Who in their right minds wouldn't want to substitute the smell of melting rubber waders for the pleasure of shade and active fish on the southwest banks of the lake? Upon our arrival the fish immediately showed their appreciation of Jim's fly tying skills by shredding our flies. We caught more trout than we could count, all of them between eight and 13 inches long. Floating lines with 10 feet of four- to six pound leader should do the trick as long as you tie on a yellow Soft Hackle, size 10 or 12. The retrieve we use is line stripped very fast in eight to 10 small (four- to six-inch) strips then a pause for about five seconds before repeating the strip.

We think you will get a kick out of catching the fish at Badger Lake, watching their antics as they chase, miss and finally take. Friends have reported catching a few big fish in this lake. We have not found the big ones yet but perhaps you will. You might try fishing caddis emergers, Hare's Ears, chironomids and Woolly Buggers.

Most of the road to the lake is asphalt and gravel. Only four miles of road is bad, Road 140. There is a sign prohibiting trailers from using 140. Nothing ventured nothing gained! Bring a tent and you will be able to camp in a beautiful primitive campground near the lake. The campground has a little stream running through it. If you drive past the campground the road will take you to the lake. You may camp closer to the lake in primitive areas. Some people boat across the lake and camp in primitive sites on the other side of the lake.

This is a remote lake and would be a perfect place for beginners learning to tube and fly fish. They would have no problem catching trout during the hatch which starts about 11:00 a.m. in July. You will need a boat or floating device of some sort as trees surround most of the lake.

In late summer and fall the water recedes in the lake. This makes the fish more available to fisherman. Launch your tube from an area with the least amount of mud and start fishing.

You will find this lake by taking Highway 26 through Sandy, Oregon and turning right onto Highway 35. Drive about four miles on Highway 35 and turn right at White River Recreational Parking Area. From the parking lot, follow Road 48 or White River Road for about 15 miles. Turn left at the second sign you see for Badger Lake. In a short distance you will turn left again and be on blacktop, Road 4860. Follow 4860 for about 7.3 miles. When the road makes a Y, go to the right onto Road 140. It is four miles to the lake.

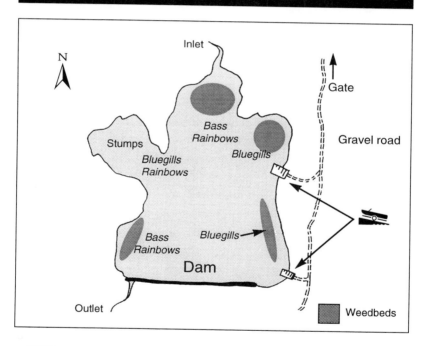

Barnes Butte Lake

*B*arnes Butte is a beautiful 40-acre lake. The first time I saw it I fell in love. Wouldn't it be a "died and gone to heaven" job living at and caring for a lake?

In the early morning hours you can see large trout jumping and watch the deer hike down from the hills to get long drinks of water. If you take the time to walk along the bank you may find a fawn that a mother has hidden in the brush while she browses nearby. You may stumble upon a pile of duck feathers and bones that are the remnants of a coyote's midnight snack. Wild geese nest on the rocky hills surrounding the lake and they honk noisily as they bring their young down to the water for lessons in survival. The young appear to need lessons in manners as well. I've watched them dive right into the middle of the salad bar, tossing and mixing it with bills and feet.

Barnes Butte Lake not only has baby fish for the geese to chase; it harbors big hungry fish for you to catch. Bluegills the size of a large man's hand will dine on any fly that is hatching as long as it is near the banks and weedbeds during the summer months. Be sure to try a Cate's Turkey, green and brown Caddis Nymphs, green Teeny Nymph and my favorite fly, a Carey Special. Did you know that the state record bluegill came out of this lake? It weighed in at 2 pounds, 10 ounces. The large bluegills at Barnes Butte can easily weigh over a pound. These fish are fun to catch because they have a knack for turning their bodies sideways so it becomes more difficult for you to pull them in.

This lake is an excellent place for a novice as well as an advanced fly fishing person to fish. My daughter is not an avid fly fisher. She fishes to spend quality time with her mother and float around the water on an air mattress on a warm sunny day. On one hot day Leslie brought a fly rod out with her on the mattress. After she had enough sun bathing she sat up straddling the mattress and while attempting to keep her balance, cast her flies at the weeds near the shore. She fished with a Carey Special and caught more bluegills than she could count. When she grew tired of catching fish she went back to catching rays, enjoying her perfect day in her own way. I have learned not to force my love for fishing onto others. Invite them to tag along with you a couple of times and allow them to do their own thing. If they don't care for the outdoors do yourself a favor and leave them at home. Both parties will be happier doing the things they enjoy most and neither will need to feel any guilt.

Largemouth bass are always eager eaters at this lake. You will have success using green Soft Hackles, green Woolly Buggers and the Gray

Hackle Peacock.

The five- to six-pound rainbow trout seem to like the Royal Bucktail Coachman, black, green and brown Woolly Buggers in sizes 4 through 10. Black and brown Woolly Buggers seem to work best for us. The trout are fighters that make fishing dreams come true. I can almost guarantee that your arm will need a sling after a day of catching these fish.

Some of the prey inhabiting this lake are midges, mayflies, pink shrimp, scuds, leeches and damselflies.

In late September and October fish lightly weighted minnow patterns and streamers in shallow water as well as the deeper water. You can catch fish on an intermediate sinking line in the deeper water of the lake and fish a slow sinker or floating line in the shallower depths.

Barnes Butte Lake is about a 2 1/2 hour drive from Sandy, Oregon. In order to find this perfect lake from Sandy, take Highway 26, following it into Prineville. In Prineville turn left on Main Street to Barnes Butte Road. Turn right onto Barnes Butte Road and drive 1.2 miles. The gate to enter the lake will be on the right. Roger Hudspeth will meet you at this point. His lake opens on March 15 and closes on October 15. You will find outhouses around the lake and plenty of shade trees where you can eat a quick lunch before hurrying back to the water.

If you want to have a great birthday suggest that your family give you a certificate to fish Barnes Butte Lake for a day. This is a gift any angler would enjoy. We guarantee you will never forget a fishing trip to Barnes Butte Lake. For further information on fees and reservations call (503) 447-4400, or write to Roger Hudspeth at P.O. Box 604, Prineville, Oregon 97754.

Clear Lake

Clear Lake may not receive an award for the most beautiful lake in Oregon but it is a great lake to fish in. A plus for this lake is that in some places you can camp right next to the water in primitive camping areas. You will also find improved campsites and restrooms

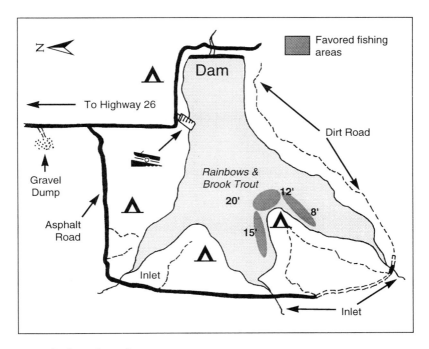

near the boat launch.

You can reach Clear Lake by taking Highway 26 east from Sandy, Oregon. Driving the speed limit for about 30 minutes from Sandy you will be at the Clear Lake Campground sign. Turn right onto Forest Service Road 2630. Follow this road straight to the lake's boat ramp, dam, restrooms and camping areas.

After turning onto Forest Service Road 2630, turn right at .8 of a mile onto the first asphalt road to your right to drive around at least half of the lake and enjoy primitive camping at more isolated spots. Driving around the lake you will find many spurs running down to the lake from the main road. If you drive 1.9 miles on this road you can turn left and drive down a dirt and gravel road right next to the water and have access to many good fishing areas. To give you a reference point we usually fish off a point at the opposite end of the dam.

Many areas of this lake are quite shallow. You may launch your tubes anywhere along the shoreline. Look for the least muddy area where you can enter the water. In the spring you will be fishing in six to

20 feet of water. By late summer or early fall it will be difficult to find any water other than what is in the main channel. This is one lake we do not fish in the fall when the water is low. When I say "low" I mean so low you must go and see it for yourself. We can't believe anyone in their right minds would allow a lake to be drained as low as we have seen this one. We find it more pleasant fishing at other reservoirs in the fall as they offer more water with easier and cleaner access.

The fishing can be excellent at this lake, weather permitting. In the spring we have fished in a snowstorm. The weather can change quickly and this seems to turn the fish off and on the bite continuously. Bugs can be hatching one minute; in the next minute the clouds can cover the sun, the air turn cold and the bugs stop hatching. Rain and wind can sweep in rapidly, too. Do not let these little storms find you out in the center of the lake in your tube. This time of year we stay nearer to the shore. If the water gets rough you can usually go to the bank and wait out a short storm. Between spring storms you will definitely appreciate the feel of warm sunshine on your back.

In the summer the weather is much more stable, pleasant and predictable. We catch fish on black and green Soft Hackles (sizes 12-16), Gray Hackle Peacocks (size 12), Black Midges (size 16), olive Woolly Buggers (size 12), brown Woolly Buggers (size 8), olive Soft Hackles lightly weighted (size 8), green and tan winged Caddis Emergers (size 8). Use the appropriate retrieve for the smaller nymphs. The retrieve that has worked best for us for the larger or bottom fly is six to eight pulls in six-inch strips, followed by a five to eight second pause. Be sure to fish the Silver Minnow as well as trying other minnow patterns using the minnow retrieve. We fish with a floating line and 10 to 12 feet of leader.

Clear Lake is well stocked in the summer and there are usually some nice sized holdover fish. You will catch brookies up to 15 inches and rainbows from 10 to 15 inches. We have friends who have caught rainbows up to 18 and 20 inches.

Bank fishing can be very exciting at Clear Lake. We have watched fish being caught with great frequency by bait fishermen using worms and marshmallows with a sinker holding the bait on the bottom. Some people even use WD-40 sprayed liberally onto the baits.

Boat fishermen have shown great curiosity and courtesy to us in our float tubes. Due to the noise of their motors we can usually over-hear their speculations as to what we are wearing under the water. We have overheard some pretty funny conversations. The favorite question for them to ask is, "Are you cold?"

You may wonder why I even show any interest in what bank and boat fishermen catch fish on? This story should explain my interest. I was first introduced to this lake by an acquaintance who is not a fly fisherman. Fritz and his friend Robert took my husband and me out for a boat ride to share their knowledge of Clear Lake with us. Thanks to them I have spent many hours at Clear Lake catching fish when there were no visible hatches. They gave me some ideas about the colors and baits that worked well for them and I transferred that knowledge apply-ing what I could to fly fishing. If silver spinners work for them I fish my Silver Minnow Patterns. If they troll something green behind their boat and it catches fish I fish green Woolly Buggers or green minnows stripped fast. If bankers are knocking the fish dead on worms I will try a brown leech pattern or Woolly Buggers.

You can improve your catch rate by being open minded to ideas from every type of fishing expert. You would not believe the good infor-mation you can obtain from people who fish differently than you. They are friendly and more than willing to give you a lesson in lake history. Don't forget to offer the boat or bank fishing person a fly to fish under his bobber when the fish are consuming hatching insects. Thanks again, Robert and Fritz, for taking the time to build a helpful, friendly bridge.

Frog Lake

*J*im informed me that Frog Lake was a good brown trout lake so I wanted to try my hand at catching these fish. On several trips to this lake we did not have a depth finder so we dragged around our

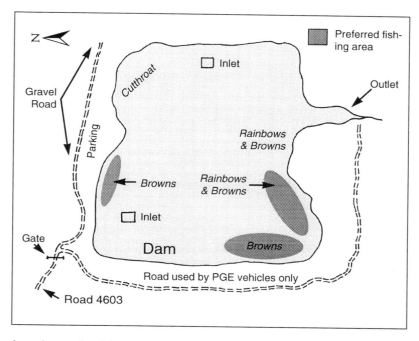

heavily weighted lines and Woolly Buggers on the way to specific bank fishing areas. We thought we were fishing on or at least near the bottom of the lake but we could never figure out why we couldn't get hits in this deeper water. This fact really bothered us since we believe in our nymph fishing techniques.

After a day of fishing at Harriet Lake we stopped by Frog Lake only to discover that someone had removed the plug. The water in the lake was missing; all that was left was a deep hole. Suddenly we understood why our heavily weighted lines and flies seemed ineffective. This lake is so deep your fly would need to rent a diving bell to get down to the bottom. We had to laugh at ourselves and our feeble attempts to fish Woolly Buggers on the bottom of this lake. Portland General Electric workers trucked many of the fish to Harriet Lake leaving some holdover fish in a pond while they plugged the leaks in Frog Lake.

There are at least two Frog Lakes on Mount Hood. We are going to talk about the lower Frog Lake near the Timber Lake Job Corps. Take Highway 224 east from Estacada until you see a sign for Road 4630 about 23 miles from Estacada. Turn left on Road 4630 and drive 2 1/2 miles on gravel road to the lake. The lake will be on the right side of the road. Park on the outside of the gate and walk in to the lake. Try running to the lake after you park your car in order to work up some extra body heat. You will need it. This is one cold lake. Wear cold water gear here all summer, at least from the waist down. It is a very short walk or run. You may launch anywhere along the bank.

There is a road around two-thirds of the lake which is not for public vehicles. The water in the lake seems to fluctuate very little. When the lake is at its fullest you can cast from the middle of the road that goes around the lake, fishing the water 10 yards from the bank. This works out well since we catch most fish near the banks. Jim was fishing from the road one evening and watching the swallows pick some type of insect off the water. A swallow decided his size 12 Mosquito looked like a great meal. Jim was shocked when his line took off into the sky. You should have seen Jim's face as that bird took line off his reel. That had to be the catch of the day!

We have never seen large hatches on Frog Lake. The fact that the water temperature is cold and the lake is deep leads us to fish the surface of the water near the bank areas. Due to these conditions the hatches seem to be in short supply and you will normally not see a lot of fish rising. Don't worry—you can still catch fish.

Use a floating line casting near shore. Fish evenings. A size 8 Muddler Minnow works well. We fish it as a large imitation insect such as a grasshopper. It also functions as a strike indicator. You can tie a four-foot dropper line on and fish a size 12 orange Tied-Down Caddis on the dropper. The majority of the fish will take the Tied-Down Caddis. The take often seems to be in slow motion. The Muddler Minnow will slowly begin to sink out of sight. When the Muddler starts sinking it is time to set the hook.

You will not have to worry about twitching your fly as long as the wind is blowing. The lake is not well protected from the wind. The wind blowing across the surface of the water will usually create enough action to move the fly.

The best fishing window will be the last hour of the evening. You can go earlier but the fish do not seem to be as active. Almost any dry fly will work in the evenings. A size 12 Mosquito or Adams will be effective. Other flies that have taken the browns, rainbows and cutthroat are Cate's Turkey (size 10), yellow Tied-Down Caddis (size 14) and a black Woolly Worm with a red tail. We have found most of the rainbows and cutthroat on the northeast end of the lake. This is where the water enters Frog Lake piped down the hill from Harriet Lake. I like to walk around the bank casting minnows and dry flies in the autumn. A green minnow pattern, size 4-6 has caught numerous fish.

There are no picnic sites or outhouses at this lake. The lake is used to power the Three Lynx generators.

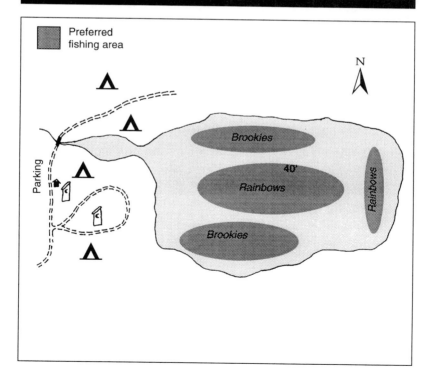

*U*nder what conditions would someone in their right mind drive three hours one way to go fishing in a lake for a day? The answer is when the lake is full of hungry rainbows and brook trout dying to play with the flies on the end of your line. We are talking about Gold Lake, a fly fishing only lake.

To reach the lake from Portland take I-5 south toward Eugene. Staying on the freeway past Eugene look for the Exit No. 188A, Oakridge and Highway 58. Taking this exit stay on 58 through the town of Oakridge. In Oakridge, fill up on great homemade cooking at Manning's restaurant. About 26.7 miles on the other side of Oakridge there will be a sign on the left side of the road for Gold Lake. Turn left off Highway 58 and drive one mile to the campground. The campground is well maintained with clean outhouses, picnic tables, fire boxes and many campsites. There are even a few camping spaces available right on the lake. There is a boat launch but don't bring your boat motor: no motors are allowed on this lake.

We found this information hard to believe but the limit for brookies is 30 a day. The rainbows are catch and release only. The Department of Fish and Game has decided that they want the lake to be a rainbow fishery only. We really can't understand why when the brook trout have some size to them and are so much fun to catch. Maybe Mother Nature will see to it that there are plenty of brookies left to spawn in here each year. The brookies are up to 16 inches and the rainbows are even larger. We have caught them up to 21 inches and we are sure there are many larger than that. All of the fish in this lake are thick and fat.

The deepest water appears to be at the farthest end of the lake from the campground. Three-quarters of the way to the end of the lake we found water 40 feet deep. It could be deeper at the end. In the spring we prefer the five to 10 foot shallow water surrounding the bank areas near the campground end of the lake.

There are several ways to fish this lake. You will see fly fishermen in boats and tubes fishing the deeper water with fast, full sinking lines or sink tips. They cast their lines and wait for them to sink completely.

Then they begin retrieving the line. The retrieve is either fast short strips or long one- to three-foot strips brought in very slowly and steadily. They seem to catch more rainbows fishing this way. The second way to fish is with a floating line working the shallow water. We fish floating lines in the spring, working the five to 10 feet of water near the shallow shore areas fairly close to the last campsite on the lake. In the summer you will catch larger fish using a sinking line in deeper water but you can still have fun catching fish on the floating line in the shallows.

We fished this lake two or three weeks after trout season opened. They had just plowed the road to the lake. We camped and woke up the next morning to a snow storm. We were frozen but determined to fish. We stayed out as long as we could stand the cold weather and finally had to give up and go home. The snow accumulation was two inches by that time. Before you make a spring run to this lake call the Forest Service and make sure the road is plowed and open.

When we came to the lake for the first time we knew nothing about how to catch fish here. We walked to the water's edge and started making our discoveries about insect activity. The most important finds were damselfly nymphs. That would be our most productive fly the entire fishing season, coupled with a dry flying ant pattern.

After fishing in this lake we have decided that it has the most hatches of any lake we have ever fished except for Crane Prairie. No matter what the weather conditions there are tons of hatches coming off almost continually. The problem is that most of the insects are very small. Dig out your small nymphs and dries. A size 14-16 dry Black Midge or a small mosquito pattern work fairly well in the evenings. When these hatches take place the fish will not bother hitting other larger flies on your line. Occasionally they will take brown, black or green damsel or dragonfly nymphs. Use sizes 6-8 Woolly Buggers in brown, green and black. The green damselfly we fish is a size 12. We have taken many fish on a size 10 Cate's Turkey and a size 12 black Soft Hackle. All of the nymphs are heavily weighted. We fish a tiny size 16-14 solid brown, black or green tapered nymph with some success. You will also want to fish Caddis Nymphs, sizes 12-14, in tan or white.

On floating lines we have found that in early spring and summer the fish definitely do not like their bugs racing through the water. We have even caught fish on a Royal Bucktail Coachman while it was sitting still in the water. Guess you'd call this non-retrieve! We normally use the appropriate retrieve for the fly we are fishing but the fish here often take the bug on the pause. In the spring this lake has a great hatch of flying ants. If you are lucky enough to be fishing here when the ants are on the water, you will have the time of your life catching fish with your imitation ant.

The same techniques and flies will continue to catch fish in the summer months with the exception that the larger fish seem to prefer deeper water. Check out the center of the lake, we found an abundance of fish hanging out in this area in the autumn. Use sinking line.

This is a wonderful place to fish. You will meet nice people and can exchange flies while telling each other about the latest lakes you have fished. Come and see for yourself—we guarantee you will be glad you did.

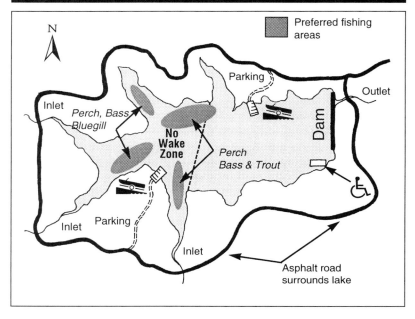

Henry Hagg Lake

*T*he only thing needed to get people hooked on fishing are a lot of cooperative fish. You will find just what the doctor ordered at Hagg Lake. If you don't want to catch a lot of perch in late summer don't bother visiting Hagg Lake. Talk about entertainment! You can be kicking along in your float tube, go through a school of perch and wind up with three fish on your line. If you look down into the water you will see 10 more chasing the fish you have caught, begging the others to jump off and give them the fly. We have caught 50 fish on this lake in a day. Hagg is an excellent fly fishing lake.

We first fished this lake on what we thought was going to be a boring summer day. We wound up having the time of our lives. On our first outing we launched our tubes at boat ramp C and facing the lake paddled to our left in about 20 feet of water all along the shoreline. We fished with an intermediate sinking line catching perch eight to 12 inches long, bluegills, bass, trout and even a bullhead. We had doubles on the bass with a size 8 green Woolly Bugger and a size 10 Zug Bug. It didn't take us long to decide that the majority of the fish in this lake were Irish. They would hit anything green in mid to late summer. Size 14 Green Scuds, sizes 14 and 12 green Soft Hackles, sizes 8-14 green Woolly Buggers, sizes 16 and 14 green chironomids and sizes 12-14 green Gold-Ribbed Hare's Ears. We also caught fish on a Red Butt Skunk (sizes 14-12) and Gray Hackle Peacock (sizes 14-12).

Fishing in the fall we turned right in our float tubes at boat ramp C and headed around the point, entering a large cove. On the far side of the cove, about 40-50 feet off shore, in 15-22 feet of water we found large fish on the screen of our depth finder. Some large fish were suspended at 10 feet while others were on the bottom 20 feet deep. I couldn't help wondering if there might not be small and largemouth bass sharing the same cove at different depths. The fish come into this cove in large numbers around 3:00 p.m. and it is a fine place to fish until near dark. We have good success with a size 12 orange Tied-Down Caddis and also catch a few fish on a size 12 yellow Tied-Down Caddis. Jim almost jumped out of his tube when he caught his first three-pound smallmouth bass on a size 12 orange Tied-Down Caddis.

We had no idea that the smallmouth bass in this lake were this large. Since then we have found that they are even larger!

Check out this same cove in the spring using a floating line with a long leader of 12-15 feet. Many fish come into the cove searching for warmer water and you will not believe how good the fishing can be. Big bass sun themselves next to the shore and trout prowl around the cove looking for minnows. Use brown Woolly Buggers in the spring.

This is another lake where we have seen *Hexagenia* shucks on the water. These bugs hatch primarily in the evening and they are big flies. They can be approximately an inch long. Try a Matt's Fur in sizes 4-6 if you can't find an imitation *Hexagenia* at the fly shop. When fish hit a fly this size they hit it hard enough to break your leader. We have broken off many fish using 6-pound (3X) tippet in this lake and suggest that you fish with a stronger 1X or 2X leader at Hagg. We have also seen the *Hexagenia* hatch sporadically during the day.

There are generally chironomid shucks on the water for the entire day. Even on cloudy days we find black chironomids and green chironomids with black heads, sizes 12-14, hatching.

We have found the basic key to success at this lake is in the fly color and the strip. When the water is very warm make two sharp six- to eight-inch strips on the line while trolling extremely slowly. Pause and repeat until three-quarters of your line is in your lap. Now let the line slide back out wagging your rod tip from side to side. After your line is back out you will repeat the strip again.

In cooler water conditions strip in line with three or four sharp jerks and pause for about six seconds. A slow hand twist retrieve also works when the water temperature drops. The bass at this lake will have a tendency to simply stop your line so you don't know if you have a snag or fish. Set the hook every time your line stops. If you catch a stump you can grumble but if it is a bass you won't have any regrets.

We found different species of fish to be hanging out together in their own hometown shore areas. Facing boat ramp C and paddling to the left there are bass under the docks and perch down from the boat ramp. At the first or second cove weed beds harbor bluegill and farther along we found more bass. We have also found a lot of bluegills around the docks at both boat ramps in late fall just before the lake closes. The trout are usually caught a little farther from the shore in the deeper water. The bullheads are just hanging out here and there. The bullhead I caught was on a size 8 green Woolly Bugger.

You will find some big rainbow trout in this lake. We have caught them in almost all areas of the lake. People have informed us that if you fish down by the dam you will also hook large trout and bass. In our tubes we do not have an inclination to fish along with the power boats pulling water skiers or to snuggle up to the many bank fishermen by the dam. It looks too crowded and rough down there for us. We fish where there are no skiers allowed and there is a "no wake" rule for boats. Most boaters comply with this rule. The police hand out tickets to boaters who don't follow the rules.

The lake is a multiple day use area with picnic tables, boating, swimming, water skiing, hiking, biking and fishing. They close the gates to the boat ramp, picnic and parking areas just before dark. You should be off the lake and on the other side of the gates when it is closing time. There is also a police boat to chase you away when it is time to leave the water. The park opens in late April on the opening day of trout season and closes in October. It is open from sunrise to sunset. There is a daily fee for park usage or you can buy a season pass. Have one or the other displayed on your windshield to avoid being ticketed.

This is the lake where I first discovered what Jim called "mud fishin". Use either floating or sinking line both work you just have to strip sinking line a lot faster. Tie on a brown or green Woolly Bugger or minnow and cast right onto or next to the shore. Start stripping and hold on because the hit will come.

I started this manner of fishing in the fall of 1993 and found it to be successful at other lakes as well. The bass and perch are happy to chase in 6 inches to four feet of water. I can hardly wait to see if this method also works in the spring!

This lake is west of Forest Grove just off Highway 47. We will let you dig out a map for this one as you will need to seek the closest route from where you live. There are too many optional routes for us to choose one for you.

Harriet Lake

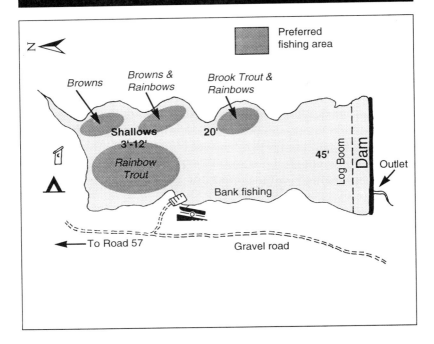

It will take you 45 minutes to reach this narrow 23-acre lake from Estacada, Oregon. Take Highway 224 just past Ripplebrook Campground. After passing the campground turn left onto Road 57 and follow Road 57 for 6.2 miles. At 6.2 miles you will cross a bridge and immediately turn left. Follow the road until you bump into the campground and lake. We generally stop at the campground restrooms (these are the only available restrooms) and then drive up to the boat ramp to park and launch our float tubes.

Facing the lake at the boat ramp, the left side of the lake is the shallow area. The deepest section of the lake is at the dam where the water is 45 feet deep. The most success we have had fishing Harriet Lake is in the shallow water area. The depth ranges from six to 15 feet becoming shallower near the banks and into the Oak Grove Fork of the Clackamas which feeds water into this lake. We have caught many rainbow trout in this section of the lake on sinking and floating lines with 10 to 12 feet of four- to six-pound leader. We use slightly weighted brown Woolly Buggers (size 8), Gold-Ribbed Hare's Ears (size 12), Gray Hackle Peacock (size 12) and green bodied, tan winged Caddis Emergers (sizes 8-10).

Bait fishermen usually fish from the bank past and above the boat ramp. You will notice the wide areas on the side of the road for parking. In the summer the parked cars collect an inch of dust. People do catch fish from the bank but I think the social atmosphere is probably as important as the fishing. We don't find it too difficult getting past them when we are going to fish in other areas of the lake. We generally cut across the lake to avoid stressing out anyone on the bank. Have you noticed that fishermen are territorial?

Harriet is stocked regularly all summer and is a very popular place to fish. After it is stocked with the small rainbows it does get harder to catch the larger fish. We are guessing that some of the larger rainbows move down to the dam area where the water is deeper to enjoy their summer vacations. If these fish enjoy cold water they have found the right lake. You will need to wear something warm under your waders even in the summer. We have almost turned into blocks of ice in the spring and fall. Dress warmly!

You can find big brown trout at the mouth of the Oak Grove Fork where it enters the lake beginning in March and through fall. The brown trout like this area of the lake. They feed on a fantastic stonefly hatch and other hatching insects at the Oak Grove Fork end of the lake. You can't help noticing all the thick bottom lake weeds for fish to hide in right off the shore where the water is shallow and calm on the lake side of the Oak Grove Fork. The brown trout are a wary fish and easily spooked but they do feed over these weed beds in the evenings. You wouldn't believe how carefully they select the insects before they take them off the top of the water. We watched one fish pass up two insects before choosing to eat the third. He actually came up under the insects and looked them over before choosing which one he wanted to eat. We wondered if he thought the other two were imitation flies.

In October or later on toward winter when the browns start their spawning we catch them on brown Woolly Buggers and minnow patterns. They will also hit spinners this time of year. The brook trout are also fall spawners; they become very aggressive in the fall. We always marvel at the beautiful colors of the brook trout when he begins to spawn. His stomach turns red and his spots almost glow. We have caught brookies, large rainbows and cutthroat around the lake but not in any one specific area. One place to look for large brookies or browns is on the far side of the lake by the log boom stretched across the lake. On the other side of the log boom towards the dam there is some deep water off a rock wall. We have taken a few meaty rainbow trout at this location.

You will find good midge hatches, a few *Callibaetis*, a little gray mayfly, caddis, dragonflies and damselflies on this lake. A size 10 Zug Bug has proved its worth as well as a size 16 Pheasant Tail Nymph fished just under the surface of the water. You may need a strike indicator on your line when fishing some of these smaller flies because the fish seem to slurp them up carefully and it is hard to detect the movement of line with your eyes.

At first glance the lake may not look like much but if you start float tubing around it you will find a pretty little cove with a small creek that meanders down the hill into the lake. This is a cool refreshing spot on a hot summer day. Paddling on down towards the dam you will also find another shallow water area strewn with debris. We have seen many fish rising here in the evenings.

Except for being able to count on catching stocker trout this lake can prove to be a challenge. If a challenge is what you are looking for you can at least start out in the right areas with the right flies. The big fish are sometimes difficult to catch. If you arrive at this lake at the right time you will never forget the experience of having a monster fish trying to drag you and your tube wherever he wants to take you.

Haystack Reservoir

 aystack Reservoir is surrounded by short scrub pine and there are amazing rock formations on the west side of the lake. A

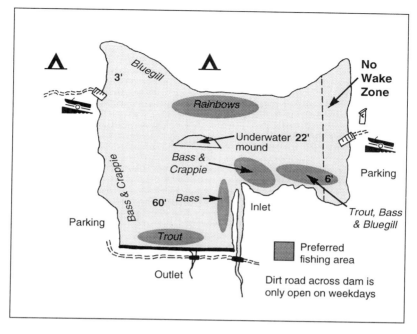

super force certainly pushed and shoved these huge rock tables around. The rocks are so impressive to see that we feel they alone are worth a trip to the lake. To get to this lake from Sandy, Oregon take Highway 26 over Mt. Hood and head toward Madras. Outside of Madras leave Highway 26 by going straight ahead at the Y to Highway 97. Follow Highway 97 for 7.6 miles. At the sign for Haystack Reservoir turn left and drive for 1.2 miles. Turn right and follow the signs to the lake. Park in the paved parking lot and walk 40 or 50 feet to the lake, launching from the shore or boat ramp.

We know that you may notice that this isn't a super, eye-popping, beautiful lake but we are of the opinion that if there is a puddle of water containing fish it is indeed a beautiful place. We enjoy fishing this lake and the fish have days when they are extremely friendly to fishermen.

Most of the camping takes place on the east side of the lake. Here the shore slopes gently into the water which makes it easy for you to walk out about 50 yards before you are in water up to your knees. Jim has fished this area with a floating line and *Callibaetis* nymphs and has had good success catching fish. He feels about this lake the way I feel about Timothy Lake. Even though at both lakes we have had many big fish break us off, neither one of us loves the other's favorite lake. We do agree on using a heavier leader when fishing Haystack. We have seen pictures of 10-pound trout taken out of this lake.

We have only fished one day on this lake when the weather was anything but perfect. (Bear in mind we aren't hard to please!). On one trip we were fishing the center of the lake and the weather was sunny, warm and beautiful. The wind came up out of nowhere and we were rolling on top of the waves. At first the rod tip would be underwater and on the roll of the next wave it would be three feet out of the water. Our tubes would plop down off the top of a large wave.

The boats all raised anchors and took off for the boat ramp. Their anchors wouldn't hold so they couldn't stay and fish. They were afraid of scratching their expensive rigs on the rocks. If I had that much money invested I would have left too. We paddled for the bank and placed ourselves in a nice safe position about 30 feet from shore and started catching big crappie and bass. We eventually had to leave the water due to tired legs from trying to hold our fishing position against the force of the wind. We took the safe route back to the car and walked along the bank. According to the boaters at the boat ramp we were the only successful fishermen on that particular day. If they could have stayed on the water they would have been successful too. We caught 15-inch fish on a black size 8 Woolly Bugger.

On the west side of the lake you will need to use an intermediate or a fast sinking line. The water is deeper on this side of the lake. A river is diverted and used to replenish the water supply in the lake as the lake water is used for irrigation. The point where the river is channeled into the lake can offer some excellent fishing. When the water is flowing into the lake it stirs up a lot of natural food and at these times we have seen many large fish on the screen of the depth finder. There is also a handicapped fishing ramp at this location on the water. This is a great fishing spot.

At Haystack you can camp very near the water which is always a plus in our book but you don't want to camp right next to the water as the water table fluctuates daily and you could awaken a little on the soggy side. If we receive a lot of rain in the spring the lake will be very high and the fishing may not be very good. We like to fish the lake in the summer when they start drawing the water down for irrigation purposes.

On one trip we were fishing near the rocks at the dam and water boatmen kept plopping down around us. They were swimming, flying off and then landing again. We had never witnessed anything like this. My fishing partner finally caught one by batting it on the head with his rod. After examining the bug we tied on a size 10 brown Tied-Down Caddis with a white head and started catching big trout. Perhaps you will want to use a size 10 Water Boatman. We know the lake is full of these little swimmers. Even though we haven't seen many dragonflies or damselflies we still catch fish on size 12 olive Woolly Buggers. We have no idea why the fish take this fly and we really don't care as long as it works. We have had serious hits on this fly. This is a good mid to late summer fly fishing lake.

Jean Lake

We were driving up a hill on Forest Service Road 3550 about 8:00 a.m. one morning when I said to Jim, "Man, does this ever look like bear country!" The words had no sooner left my mouth when a black bear went racing across the narrow, rocky, one lane road 20 yards in front of the truck. Wow! He was moving fast and didn't look one bit clumsy to me. He turned for one brief second and flashed us a toothy grin just before his big black rump jiggled over the bank and out of sight. An experience like this is worth a complete day of fishing but you won't find us turning our truck around and racing back towards home. Sights like these are the icing on the cake and if you were to follow us around for a while you'd be licking a lot of icing off the cake because we have seen awesome sights on our fishing trips.

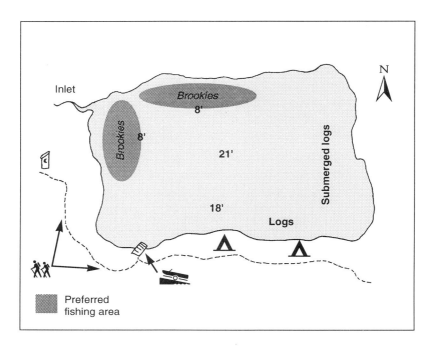

The best way to find Jean Lake from Sandy, Oregon is to remain on Highway 26 until you reach the turn off for Highway 35. Stay on Highway 35 for about six miles until you get to Bennett Pass. Turn right at Bennett Pass onto Road 240. Road 240 turns into Forest Service Road 3550. It is 6.6 miles to the lake. This is a slow road! At the fork in the road just prior to Camp Windy veer left, staying on Road 3550. Check your odometer and drive 1.3 miles. There is a small dirt road on your left. Park about 300 yards from the dirt road in a wide spot. There is a trail sign on the right side of the road marking the trail down to the lake. The trail sign is down the path a short distance from the road. This trail is about a half mile down and two miles back up. Walking down is easy. We know that at an altitude of 5,000 feet the steep trail just makes it feel like two miles hiking out. Hiking out poses no problems if you go slowly. Carry your lightest float tube.

The deepest water is in the center of the lake, 21 feet deep, so you won't need to pack in a depth finder or take a bunch of extra heavily weighted flies! You might take a camera along for pictures. On the west end of lake where you launch your float tubes the water is eight feet deep about 20 yards off the bank. The east end of the lake is about as shallow as the west end but there appear to be more logs and debris under the water and fewer weeds.

We fish the west end and north side tossing our flies near the weed beds. The south side appears to be the preferred spot for bank fishing. At least this is the only place we have ever found a bait container. The water looks deep enough to plunk. All the way down the middle of the lake and 20 yards off the bank it is 21 feet deep.

A book we read suggested that the fish in this lake would hit anything. Someone forgot to tell the fish that story. Our first trip we trolled and twitched, yanked and jerked on our intermediate sinking lines. We tried at least 15 different flies until we found a working combination of floating lines with about 10 feet of four- to six-pound test leader. We catch fish on size 12 Iron Blue Wingless, size 6 weighted brown Woolly Bugger, size 10 brown Soft Hackles, size 12 orange Tied-Down Caddis and a *Callibaetis* Nymph. The fish are rainbow trout and brookies nine to 15 inches long. The small fly retrieve is two to six quick pulls of two to four inches at a time. Pause for five to 10 seconds and repeat. Use a normal retrieve for Woolly Buggers.

From the month of September on into October wear long underwear to fish here. One day in October we had an adventure that found us fishing in a full blown rain and wind storm. We had left Portland just ahead of a storm but we had talked ourselves into believing that if we walked down into this lake we would find shelter from any storm. We enjoy fishing this lake and we could hardly wait to test our theory. When we first arrived at the lake on that memorable day we had only been in the water for 10 minutes when it started to rain. First it teased us with little droplets and a few small gusts of wind. Within 20 minutes we were trying to spin around in our tubes every few seconds to avoid the next squall hitting us full in the face. This had quickly turned into a nasty storm and the only thing in our favor was that there wasn't any lightning.

At this point Jim yelled at me over the storm, "Did you see that?" Of course I hadn't seen whatever "that" was. I was busy fishing and riding the whitecaps trying not to drown! Jim informed me that a giant water spout had lifted off the water right next to him and then released all of its liquid on top of his head. I was wondering if he was lucky enough to have found fish in his lap. He was laughing like a crazy man and wanted to know if I had gotten a picture of the water spout. I curtly informed him that I had left my rain filter at home.

Somewhere in the middle of this washing machine experience I peeked out from under my hat and spied a shadow moving through the rain. Squinting, I desperately tried to keep my eye on the spot where I had last seen the movement. When the rain let up for a brief second I could barely make out a large osprey sitting in a tree staring down at two fools on the water.

To answer the unasked question, yes you can catch fish in the middle of a monstrous storm but don't give the two of us a test to see how bright we are. We were successful using floating lines with size 12 black Nymphs and size 12 black Soft Hackles tied onto a six-pound test leader. The soggy, rocking, spinning, retrieve was the same as for a sunny day.

You will find primitive campsites surrounding the lake with one set of outhouses at the west end of the lake. It appears to us that some folks ride their horses down and around the lake area. Besides horse droppings the only other thing we have ever seen associated with another being other than a campfire ring was one empty jar of trout bait. We hope you will respect these lakes and not leave any type of trash lying around. If you see any please pick it up and pack it out, even if it isn't yours.

Kingsley Reservoir

One morning Jim and I set off to catch all of the fish in Rainy Lake. We had never been to this lake before but confidence was oozing from our pores. We knew that the fish couldn't stand a chance against us. (We develop this arrogant attitude when we have been successful catching fish a few days in a row.)

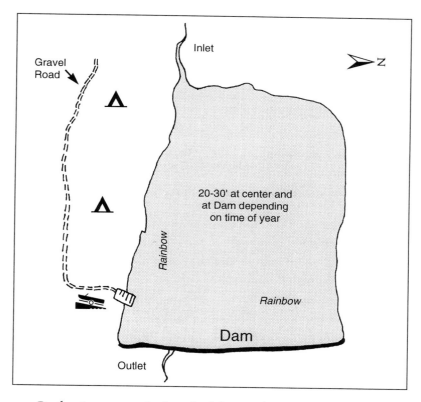

By the time we arrived at the lake we thought the fillings in our teeth had come loose due to the bumpy roads we had just driven over and it was raining. I wondered if any important pieces had fallen off the truck so after we stopped I took a quick inventory. We had parked the truck right in front of a small campground and at 9:30 a.m. the cold, damp campers weren't moving about yet. We are not exactly a quiet pair and while we were putting on our gear the campers came out of their tents to stir up soggy campfires and cast sour glances our way.

We balanced our float tubes on top of our heads and started walking down a trail to the left of the campground. At first the trail was well worn so we thought it was the right trail. Wrong. . .we had walked quite a distance when I noticed that the trail did not look as well-used as I thought it should. I started mumbling about how someone ahead of me had assured me that it was only a quarter-mile hike to the lake. I guess he must have heard me because we did an about face and went back to the campground to humbly beg for directions. The people smirked as they pointed up the hill past their tents. By the time we got up the hill we were panting and it was raining hard.

We took a minute to catch our breath as we admired the beauty for this lake. We fished for 10 minutes and then broke our own record for leaving a lake. The weather was once again against us. There were no visible hatches and neither of us wanted to stay. By the time the people from the camp had walked up the hill to see what kind of show we would put on for them in the water, we were carrying our gear back down to the car. The campers informed us that fishing had been lousy and so had the weather. We loaded the car up and drove the back roads over to Kingsley Reservoir.

To reach Kingsley Reservoir, if you live on the Portland side of Mt. Hood take I-84 east and exit at Hood River at Exit 62. After you exit the freeway turn right at the stop sign. In about 50 feet turn right again on Country Club Road. Remain on this road for 2.9 miles and you will come to another stop sign. Turn right, still on Country Club Road. In 1.8 miles at yet another stop sign (the Oak Grove Store will be on the corner) turn right onto Green Point Road. In less than a block bear right on Binns Hill Drive for .2 of a mile. Turn left and follow the signs to Kingsley. This road takes you to the lake in about six miles.

Kingsley Reservoir (or Green Point Reservoir) sits at an altitude of 3,200 feet. No wind, no rain, the sun was shining and the water was covered with the slight beginnings of a nice *Callibaetis* hatch. We headed for the boat ramp, launched our tubes and started fishing. It was about 10:30 a.m. and it didn't take us long to tie a *Callibaetis* Nymph onto our dropper lines. We used floating lines with a size 10 Zug Bug on the end of our leaders and were catching stocker and holdover rainbow trout averaging 10 to 14 inches. We couldn't help thinking of what we had left behind at Rainy Lake: cold, wet, fishless folks. It is always hard for us to believe how different the weather can be just a few miles away at another lake.

Paddling around the lake we found the summer water depth to be 15 to 18 feet down at the dam. The center and edges of the lake were nine to 12 feet deep. There are quite a few stumps and logs under the water. This lake covers about 60 acres so it isn't very far to paddle around if you care to. Summer finds the surface area of the lake much smaller due to the irrigation of orchards.

By 12:30 p.m. the *Callibaetis* hatch had reached its peak and was starting to taper off. We switched to sinking lines and caught fish on an unweighted size 8 Woolly Bugger with a black body and brown tail. It was necessary to troll very slowly and the strip was a little different. We let out 30 to 40 feet of line, jerked in a couple of six-inch pulls, paused and repeated until we had about six feet of line brought up. Then we would release the six feet of line back into the water and start again. We were keeping the line at the exact depth the fish were swimming around or suspended.

We discovered an interesting fact at Kingsley. This is the only lake we have ever fished where people on the bank fishing Pautzke Eggs and worms, people rowing around the lake in boats using black Panther Martins and other spinners and fly fishermen were all catching fish simultaneously. It was a remarkable sight!

We have decided to tell you about spring fishing at this lake. We have had good times at this time of year. Tie on a size 16 black Chironomid, size 12 gray Soft Hackle, size 10 green or brown Woolly Bugger, size 10 orange Tied-Down Caddis or a size 10 brown Tied-Down Caddis. Fish any of these flies on floating lines using 10 to 12 feet of leader. When the fish begin homing in on a small brown caddis hatch they will take most of these flies if you present them on or near the surface of the water. We even fished a couple of these flies dry and could watch the fish grab the fly and run off with it, letting him set the hook himself. The lake is loaded with crawdads; a size 6 brown Woolly Bugger works well, too.

There are numerous primitive campsites but no drinking water available. Near the boat ramp you will find two newly repaired out-houses. In late summer the shore of the lake leaves a lot of room for casting from the bank. If we lived close to this reservoir and had small children we would bring them along for a day of fun catching fish.

Laurance Reservoir

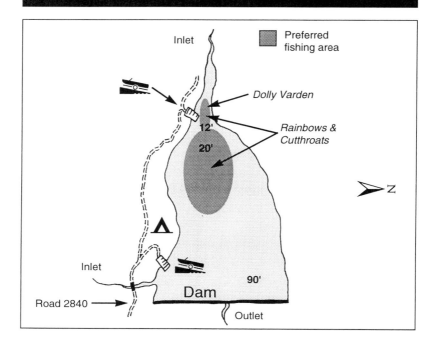

Inlet

Preferred fishing area

Dolly Varden

Rainbows & Cutthroats

12'

20'

N

Inlet

90'

Road 2840 →

Dam

Outlet

*L*awrence, Laurance or Laurence—any way you spell the name it is a fantastic fishing hole! We decided to use the spelling that was on the road sign directing us to the lake. We figured the local population should know how to spell the name of their own lake.

The fishing regulations for the lake were changed in 1992. It is now a fly and lure fishery only and you are not allowed to keep Dolly Varden or any fish with unclipped fins. Electric trolling motors are permitted. We feel that the new rules will do nothing but enhance the fishing at Laurance Lake.

The trip to the lake is about a one hour drive from Sandy, Oregon. You can find the lake if you take Highway 26 to Highway 35. Drive about 22.4 miles on Highway 35 until you see the sign for Parkdale and Dee on the left side of the road. Turn left at this sign. In .5 of a mile turn left again at Culbertson Road. Remain on Culbertson Road for 1.2

miles until you come to a second stop sign. Turn left on Clear Lake Drive. You will see the sign for the lake in 1.7 miles. Turn right at the sign onto Road 2840. Drive four miles on a good asphalt road that will lead you directly to the lake. This road offers a nice view of the Hood River side of Mt. Hood which Portlanders don't see daily. You might want to bring a camera.

You will approach the dam end of the lake first. There is a boat ramp near the dam and the campground host's tent or trailer. There are two outhouses at this campground. Drive past the campground until you approach a boat ramp next to the road on your right. You will be fishing the west end of the lake. Parking above the ramp, you can walk down to the boat ramp and launch your tube.

We fish where the little creek above the boat ramp enters the lake. We have caught Dolly Varden here on yellow Tied-Down Caddis close to the shore. Use a floating line in this shallow area. For rainbow and cutthroat trout we fish from the boat ramp all the way across the lake about 100 yards down from the boat ramp. We troll around this entire end section of the lake in our tubes catching fish on floating and intermediate sinking lines. In the spring and early summer we fish around the bushes in the shallow area of water and catch many fish on floating lines using a size 14 March Brown Nymph, sizes 10-12 weighted black, brown or olive green 1X long Woolly Buggers, size 12 dark brown Gold-Ribbed Hare's Ear, tan or yellow Caddis Emergers and Spruce Flies retrieved in long, slow strips. The retrieves we use on the nymphs in the spring are the same as for summer. Don't do anything too fast at this lake. If you aren't catching fish try a line twitch, change flies or make your leader 2 to 5 feet longer.

For summer and spring the retrieve we use for fishing nymphs is two to eight short quick, three- to six-inch strips followed by a five second pause and repeat. For Woolly Buggers use one or two long slow 12-inch pulls and an occasional sharp twitch before releasing the line back into the water. Wait a few seconds and give it a couple of small strips. Let the fly rest for five seconds and repeat. In the summer we found fish hitting the brown bugger if we let the fly settle back down after a long strip. We troll very slowly. When the water warms you will need to slow down even more, not trolling, barely moving in your tube. This is one lake where we have never been skunked but we know only too well that there can always be a first time! More flies that work for us at Laurance in the summer are yellow Tied-Down Caddis (sizes 8-10), brown Woolly Buggers (sizes 8-6), Carey Specials (size 10), *Callibaetis* (size 16), orange Tied-Down Caddis (size 10) and Gray Hackle Peacocks (size 12).

One day at this lake we changed flies every hour or so in order to continue catching fish the whole day. We don't know if the fish became accustomed to seeing the same flies or if the changes were due to varied hatches. We would go from brown Woolly Buggers to green Woolly Buggers to black Woolly Buggers and back to brown or green and black again. It was strange! The fish would consistently hit the different colors. I guess if this story needs a moral it would be change your flies when the fish quit hitting.

This is one of the first lakes Jim and I fished after we started fishing together. I had little or no knowledge of how to fly fish or what species of fish I had on when I caught one. What I did grasp from Jim's fishing lessons was how and when to set the hook. I was good at that.

When I fly fish I enjoy a little solitude. One sunny July day I had paddled my tube away from Jim to fish by myself when suddenly I hooked a beautiful, strong 16-inch fish. I yelled at Jim trying to describe the fish to him. Since we were so far apart and I didn't want to injure the fish I let the big bruiser slip back into the lake where he belonged. I knew I would probably catch many more just like him. Wrong! I had caught a Dolly Varden and neither of us caught another Dolly on that particular day. Jim paddled over and pumped me for information until he was totally satisfied regarding the species and method I had used to catch the fish. He tied on a Yellow Caddis and began flogging the water. He still didn't catch a Dolly Varden. I chalked the Dolly up to beginner's luck.

One morning at the lake we started out by fishing size 6 brown Woolly Buggers on the end of the leader. The droppers we used were a yellow Caddis Fly and a Gray Hackle Peacock. From 9:00 to 11:00 a.m. the fish completely ignored the Woolly Bugger and hit the dropper flies.

At 11:00 a.m. they reversed their feeding on small insects and would only take Woolly Buggers. Had we used the wrong flies it would have been easy to say the fish weren't hitting that day.

In our fishing experience we have found that fish will usually strike if you offer them what they want. It is a matter of figuring out what is on their daily menu. As soon as you find out if they want pizza with or without all of the toppings, hot dogs, hamburgers with or without relish, ketchup, onions or mustard on any given day and at any given time you will probably catch fish. We hope you use our basic fish catching knowledge of this lake as a springboard to discover other flies that will catch fish for you.

We are sure that by now you are aware that any lake can become quite windy. One day the wind was blowing about 25 miles an hour when we arrived. We got ready to launch but Jim discovered he had forgotten his fins. The choice was simple: either leave him on the bank to suffer alone, whining and gnashing his teeth or lash our tubes together and each of us put one of my fins on an outside foot. We did the latter. We always laugh and have fun fishing but this day was especially hilarious. The fish started hitting our offerings immediately. We think it was because they wanted a free ride to the surface to laugh at the two crazy people.

We also made the following remarkable discoveries about "double tubing":

1. One of us couldn't stop kicking just because the other person was tying on a fly or we would go in circles.

2. It was much easier to check out and eat the other person's snacks.

3. Two tubes would have to backtrack if one fly became hung up on a stump.

4. We had to kick in unison to have any control.

5. One leg starts wearing out after a couple of hours.

The wind was a double hindrance, creating more hard work for us. If we stopped kicking it would blow us back toward the dam away from where we had planned to fish and exit at the boat launch. After we had been catching fish like this for about an hour a boat with two curious fishermen anchored close enough to observe us but not close enough for us to reach them. We were busy laughing and catching as the strong fish continued to jump over our partner's line and wrap themselves around our legs. We are certain we were a comical sight. The men had no idea about what was going on under the water with our fins. This made us laugh even harder. We assumed that the two men must have surmised that we were Siamese twins, crazy or on drugs.

When we decided to call it quits for the day we struggled out of our tubes, each of us dragging one very tired leg back up the boat ramp. With stomach and face muscles sore from laughter we tucked another memorable fishing day under our belts and headed back home. The joy and memories of this day would have been lost forever if we hadn't possessed some extra strapping, a little ingenuity and a lot of patience and creativity.

Olallie Lake

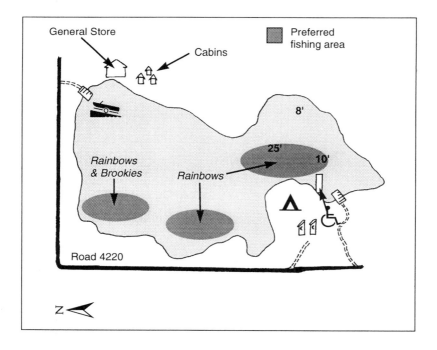

*T*here are many lakes in the Olallie Lake area. You need to get out your map and take a look because it is hard to believe that there can be so many places to fish so close to each other. Some of the lakes in this region that you can drive right to are: Lower, First, Monon, Horseshoe and Breitenbush. Many of the other lakes will require hiking. At this writing boat motors are not allowed on any of the lakes.

There are several Forest Service Roads that will lead you to Olallie. We recommend that you buy a map because there can be a lot of zigzagging around the roads in this area. As a starting point, from Estacada, Oregon take Highway 224 east. Highway 224 will run into Road 46 just past Ripplebrook Campground. Remain on Road 46 for several miles until you turn left onto the Forest Service Road of your choice. We generally choose Road 4690 to Road 4220. On these roads you will pass several small lakes but continue on until you come to Olallie, a 240 acre lake. From Estacada allow about an hour for the trip to Olallie.

Olallie Lake is indeed the largest of the lakes in the area. It has nice camping areas but there are also plenty of good camping spaces available at the other lakes. At Olallie there is wheelchair access. A platform deck with rails has been built out over the water in a good fishing location.

This is a scenic camping area with more than enough shoulder space. When you visit these lakes take an extended vacation because it takes many weeks to fish all of these lakes thoroughly. Olallie is at an elevation of 4,900 feet with few submerged weeds. At times there seems to be a lack of abundantly hatching insects but there are still hatches even though many are minor. We have witnessed a huge evening hatch of midges with the water as dimpled as it could be in any rainstorm. We have also seen plenty of mosquitoes, a few caddis and mayflies.

Leech patterns, Woolly Buggers and minnow patterns usually work best on this series of lakes. At Olallie we hook most of our fish on sizes 8-12 brown or black Woolly Buggers using intermediate sinking lines. We prefer this line due to the frequent changes in water depth on this 240-acre lake. A small area example: Approximately a third of the way across the lake from the handicap platform the water is about nine to 10 feet deep but two-thirds across it is 16 feet deep. Near the west shore it tapers off to six to eight feet. Just off the north side of platform the water is 19-25 feet deep. The back section of the lake is fairly shallow with the deepest section 14 feet deep.

If you are going to fish in water six to eight feet deep, fish with your floating line. Use the proper retrieve for the flies you tie onto your leader. On some days fish prefer a faster strip than normal. We have pictures of friends with six-pound rainbows who swear by the Spruce Fly. We know other people who troll around the lake and pull along nightcrawlers, catching lots of big brooders. This should give you a good idea on what to start out using to catch fish.

Although most of the lakes are lacking in good weed beds Breitenbush Lake does have an abundance of weeds on the south end near the primitive camping area. This is a 60-acre lake at an elevation of 5,500 feet. Due to the weed beds at Breitenbush you will see more insects hatching. Fish a brown or olive size 8 Woolly Bugger and, of course, a Spruce Fly.

Many of the lakes in this area are fairly shallow with a few deep sections of water. Monon seems to be the most shallow over a larger section of water. Monon is a 91-acre lake at an altitude of 5,000 feet. Use your floating line on Monon and aside from using minnow patterns and leeches keep an eye open for specific hatches. We have seen midges and mosquitoes at almost all of the lakes.

Horseshoe Lake is 14 acres and the altitude is 5,400 feet. You can camp right on the lake if you get to the campground first. This lake has good access for launching float tubes and also has an outhouse. A size 8 brown Woolly Bugger has produced fish in this lake on intermediate sinking lines.

All of the lakes are well stocked with rainbows and brookies. If you drive to the north end of Olallie Lake you will find a little general store where you can buy gas, basic fishing necessities and see pictures of trout up to 10 pounds and over.

A couple of years ago Jim taught one of his friends to float tube fish. After paddling around and successfully catching fish the friend thought his boy could float tube fish. The boy was paralyzed from the waist down. The next trip the father put his son in a float tube and gave him ping pong paddles to maneuver with. The young man took to this sport like a duck to water and Jim maintains that when this kid is fishing in his tube they are all equals. The young man now fishes from a U-boat which is easier for his dad to assist him in and out of. Fishing from a float tube must make this young man feel ecstatic because it sure has that effect on us!

This entire area is well known for its hiking trails. If you plan to fish the hike in lakes, be aware that you will need a special permit to fish the lakes on the Warm Springs Indian Reservation. There is no permit required on the lakes we have mentioned above due to the fact that they are not on the Indian Reservation. Bring your fishing and camping gear, a valid fishing license, a camera and lots of vacation time!

Pine Hollow Reservoir

Preferred fishing area
Homes
Restrauant boat rentals store
Blacktop road
Trout
Bass & Crappie
12'
Bass
21'
Bluegills
Bouys
32'
30'
Dam
Outlet
Trout & Bass
Park
Inlet
Paved road

Do you want to catch some solid 16-inch trout, hand-sized bluegills and largemouth bass? If the answer to this question is "yes," Pine Hollow is the place for you. We have also heard that you can catch crappie off the north boat ramp but we have never taken the time to investigate the crappie fishing.

When the fish are cooperative we have had more fun in this lake than you can shake a rod at. Before you fish any lake always check the regulations. The reason we bring this up is because we are going to introduce you to some night fishing entertainment. Read the regulations and you will see that it is lawful in most places in Oregon to fish at night as long as you fish for a warmwater species of fish. We reiterate, always check the regulations first.

For night fishing you will want to stay near the banks. The big fish will come in to feed in the shallow water under cover of darkness. If you can't see you will know that you are close enough to the bank when you kick the bottom of the lake. For night fishing you will need a small flashlight so you can see to unhook fish and tie flies on. You need both hands free to do these tasks. We recommend you buy lights that you can wear as glasses. The type of glasses we use are frames that contain batteries with two little light bulbs attached to the frames. There is another type of fishing light made that fits over your head with a half-inch lamp but it seems to be too heavy and has a tendency to slide down your forehead. Turn your light off or remove your light glasses while you are fishing.

If you have never fished in a float tube in the dark you are in for the time of your life. The fish are going to twirl you around in circles and you will be reaching into thin air trying to locate your line with the fish somewhere on the end. The first time out you may feel a little spooky, especially if a beaver swims by and scares you to death by slapping his tail on the water. If you are afraid of the dark, bring some friends along for moral support. Your friends will thank you and you will thank us for suggesting this crazy activity. You are going to catch fish and laugh your heads off. Don't limit night fishing to this lake. Find another lake that has warmwater fish and give it a shot. Night fishing is a hoot!

One summer night excursion found Jim casting his black four- or five-inch unweighted Rabbit Leech into the weeds where he caught a stick. As his floating line tightened he set the hook, thinking it was a fish. The stick fired right back at his head knocking his hat off into the dark water. His first thought was that a mad bird was attacking him then he breathed a sigh of relief to find a stick at the end of his line.

Tie eight-pound test tippet on your line because the fish really nail these flies. If you are fishing a nearly full moon or a full moon the black leech will not work. Switch to a popper or a size 4-6 Muddler Minnow that will allow you to have a good wake trailing the fly. We troll all of the flies and with the leech pattern we also add an occasional twitch or two to the line. Twitch the line about one or two inches but do not bring any line in. You are trying to impart a little more action to the fly to attract the fishes' attention.

Aside from catching fish the sky at night becomes the largest theater screen you will ever see. Because of the lack of city lights the moon and stars appear bright and close enough for you to touch. You sense the sky surrounding you and know that you are a part of the galaxy. Listen to the call of the coyote, mumbling geese and ducks, frogs croaking and crickets chirping on the THX Sound System as you watch the show. Don't forget to hold tightly to your rod while you are at this theater.

This lake is located on the east side of Mt. Hood about 66 miles from Sandy, Oregon. Blacktop all the way. Take Highway 26 to Highway 35. Drive for about four miles on Highway 35 to the White River Recreational Area on the right side of the road. Turn right, driving into the huge parking area. This is the entrance to the White River Road or Road 48 and you are on your way to Pine Hollow via Rock Creek Reservoir. Drive 22 miles to Rock Creek Reservoir. Drive past Rock Creek and go about five miles to Wamic. At the main intersection in Wamic there is a stop sign. Go straight up the hill at the stop. The road will eventually lead you to the north boat ramp at Pine Hollow and camping facilities. If you want to go to the south boat ramp where we usually put in, turn left and drive about two miles. At the road sign for south Pine Hollow Reservoir turn right. In one mile you will be at the boat ramp. Park next to the boat ramp and start dragging out your gear.

Facing the lake on the south boat ramp and looking across the lake to the other ramp there is a deep slot of water. Depending on the time of year it could be 32 to 28 feet deep. We stay out of this area and leave it to the boats and summer water skiers. We like to launch from the boat ramp and paddle to the right, fishing the first little cove next to the boat ramp. The water in this small cove warms quickly and holds bass. When you are about 20 to 30 feet off shore the water deepens gradually from 20 to 40 feet on down to the rocks at the dam, where they pipe the water out of the reservoir. We fish the deeper water anywhere from 20 feet from the rocks out and across to the other side of the cove. This area usually has 10 to 16 inch trout cruising around. We are most productive with intermediate sinking lines in this deeper water using three to eight quick strips a couple of inches long.

Depending on the time of year and day you will catch trout on Chironomids (match color and size), yellow Tied-Down Caddis, Cate's Turkeys, Soft Hackles or Gold-Ribbed Hare's Ears. You will also catch fish in deeper water fishing minnow patterns all year. Use the proper retrieve for minnows.

Paddling over to the other side of the cove you will see land jutting out into the water. This side of the cove and around the land jutting out is where you may find many bluegills. The bluegills chase small Zug Bugs and small yellow Tied-Down Caddis. In a fishing day we often work our way on around and down near the east end of the lake. If you care to work the shallow shore areas with a dry fly tie on a Mosquito or tan Dry Caddis. Big bass chase the bluegills in the shallow water near the shore. Fish this area about 20 yards from the far side of the land jutting out and almost to the end of the lake. Sometimes you will have to put on larger flies to discourage the bluegills.

In the summer there are usually buoys in this area. We fish the shore side of the buoys, drawing an imaginary straight line running almost to the end of the lake. Normally trout lurk 20 to 40 feet off the shore in 20 to 30 feet of water. The end of the lake shallows out to three feet.

In the fall you will find many largemouth bass at the back end of the lake in the shallow warm water. You can enjoy catching them with Royal Bucktail Coachmen, Uncle Dudleys, white or green minnows or Cate's Turkeys. Use floating line and a fast strip.

The big fish fatten up for winter by eating minnows. In the fall we start fishing later in the day, arriving at the lake around 1:00-2:00 p.m. If the sun is shining and there is a hatch, the hatch will start later and the insects are usually smaller. We fish with a black Midge held down with a small weighted black Woolly Bugger and tie on a *Callibaetis* fly for a dropper at this time of year. The minnow patterns we use are size 6-8 and the other flies are sizes 10-12, except for *Callibaetis* and midges which should be size 16.

One sunny windless day the fish weren't biting and Jim and I hadn't even caught a stick. Out of sheer boredom I tied a swivel and small silver Flatfish onto my fly rod and fished this ensemble on my intermediate sinking line. I started kicking my fins like crazy and pulling my line out to the side of my tube keeping it as tight as I could in order to make my Flatfish wobble. The Flatfish wobbled and the trout started to gobble.

After I caught a few fish I decided to retie the Flatfish and accidentally knocked it off my tube. I grabbed for it and missed. My heart and the Flatfish slowly sank to the bottom of the lake. I dug around in my tube pockets, found a gold Flatfish and placed it on the end of the line. I couldn't believe my luck when the fish started chewing on it, too. My partner, who is somewhat of a fly fishing purist sat quietly, watching, shaking his head in disbelief. He informed me that the whole procedure looked like too much work for him.

By this time my leg was getting primed for a cramp and I was pooped. Jim informed me that he would sit down at his vise and tie me a new fly that night. This is how the Silver and Gold Minnows were born. We use these flies anytime the fish have a preference for minnows. They work in the summer as well as the fall. Silver has been the best color. We usually fish them on floating lines in the fall and sinking lines in the summer.

We have watched boats trolling with Ford Fenders, Flatfish and spinners as well as bank fishermen picking up fish on worms and marshmallows, spinners and Pautzke Eggs. We have been told that people ice fish here in the winter and are successful catching fish by offering them Velveeta Cheese on hooks.

There are fee campgrounds on the north side of the lake. We hope to see you on this lake on a windless, warm, bug hatching day catching cooperative fish.

Rainbow Lake

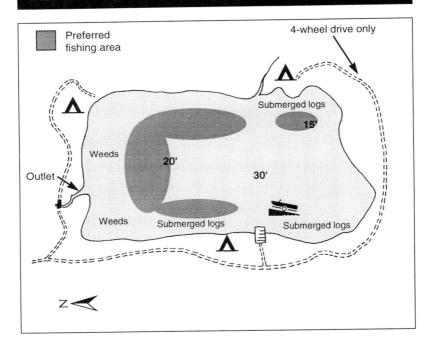

Preferred fishing area

4-wheel drive only

Submerged logs

15'

Weeds

20'

Outlet

30'

Weeds

Submerged logs

Submerged logs

N

Rainbow Lake is a picture-perfect lake sitting in a box canyon with a beautiful view of rugged Mt. Jefferson. Driving to the lake will take you about two hours from Estacada, Oregon. It is one of the most picturesque lakes that we frequent. The lake is full of big fat brookies ranging in size from 13 to 16 inches. They are good strong fighters. On a day that the bite is good you will have to stop fishing to give your wrist a rest. To our knowledge this lake is not stocked—it is self sustaining.

The hatches at Rainbow Lake are normally so abundant that the fish will not even begin to eat all of the insects on the surface of the water. You will see two or three different sizes and colors of chironomids hatching. At certain times of the year little spiders come sailing past you on six-foot strands of web searching for new surroundings. Webs will cling from your rod like tinsel on a Christmas tree. There will be days when the top of the water turns blue as brilliant damselflies zip about. You will have to shake them off your rod or it will get too heavy to hold. This is the only lake we have ever fished where the dragonflies hover in front of you looking you square in the eye to see if you measure up to their standards for a good meal. We became unnerved the first time this happened; it is indeed spooky but you will get used to it. You can watch small bright green beetles swim by your tube attempting to pass unscathed the hungry brookies. Scuds, caddisflies, leeches and crayfish become tasty treats for the fish who love to devour them. When you are ready to leave the lake you will probably need to rinse the *Callibaetis* shucks off your tube. If this sounds like a fly fishing utopia, it is—when the fish are biting.

When we first started coming to this lake we renamed it Stingy Lake. We put in many unsuccessful fishing hours until we learned how to catch fish in this lake. We would make deals with each other as to how long we would have to stay on the water and be punished by watching the fish jump all around us while only being able to catch two or three of the dumbest ones. Our determination and persistence were finally rewarded.

Rainbow Lake has an average depth of 20 feet. There are submerged trees along the shore so we fish about 10 yards off shore around most of the lake. We catch the most fish in the summer using intermediate sinking lines. We put a size 6 brown or green Woolly Bugger on as a bottom fly and use sizes 12-16 Scud Specials, size 14-16 Chironomids in red, black or copper, size 12-14 Cate's Turkeys or size 16 *Callibaetis*.

We do not fish the shallow water until spring and fall. We have discovered that on most of our lakes in the spring you will need to fish a floating line over shallow weedbeds to catch fish. On Rainbow Lake for spring fishing, fish in five to six feet of water using a size 10 brown Woolly Bugger with six wraps of .035 lead. In any season on this lake you must fish extremely slowly. The strip will vary. On one day two short two- to four-inch strips with a five second pause will catch fish. Another day you may find yourself stripping 15 short two- to four-inch strips before pausing. Don't kick fast! Kick one foot and float and in a few minutes kick the other foot. The lack of movement is essential as the water becomes warmer in the summer. In our normal summer weather conditions we find that June and July are the best months for catching fish. Be sure you practice catch and release so you will have fish to come back for. Boat and bank fishermen usually give up fishing here in the summer when the majority of fish are feeding on insects.

In order for you to reach this little gem drive east from Estacada, Oregon on Highway 224, which will turn into Road 46. Follow Road 46 all the way to Detroit Lake. When you reach the first stop sign at Detroit Lake turn left onto Highway 22. Those of you not using the Estacada route can take I-5 south and exit at Highway 22 until you reach Detroit dam. In six miles you will see a sign on the right side of the road for Cooper Ridge Road. Turn right, driving straight over the bridge and bear right after crossing the bridge. You will drive on asphalt for about three miles. Turn right onto a well-used gravel road heading up to the lake. After a few miles watch for a turn off 45 degrees to the left. (Always follow the roads that appear to be traveled the most.) The road now becomes a little less desirable. About a mile up this road take the fork to the right. As you follow the road around to the lake, stay to the left. Just before you reach the lake there will be a road to your left going around an end of the lake. Don't take this road unless you own a 4X4. Keep going straight, driving on a narrow, badly rutted lane. After about 30 yards you will arrive in the small parking area. We do not recommend this road for motor homes or trailers.

There are only primitive camping areas at Rainbow Lake and no restrooms. A car top boat or float tubes can be launched by sliding the boat or walking your tube 10 or 15 feet to the lake. Just keep in mind that the boat will have to be pulled back up to your car. If you are picky about your car perhaps you will want to drive an old vehicle on these roads. The bushes are close to the road in a couple of areas which could leave minor scratches in the vehicle's paint. If you aren't worried about a paint scratch, come up to this lake and have a super fishing experience.

Rock Creek Reservoir

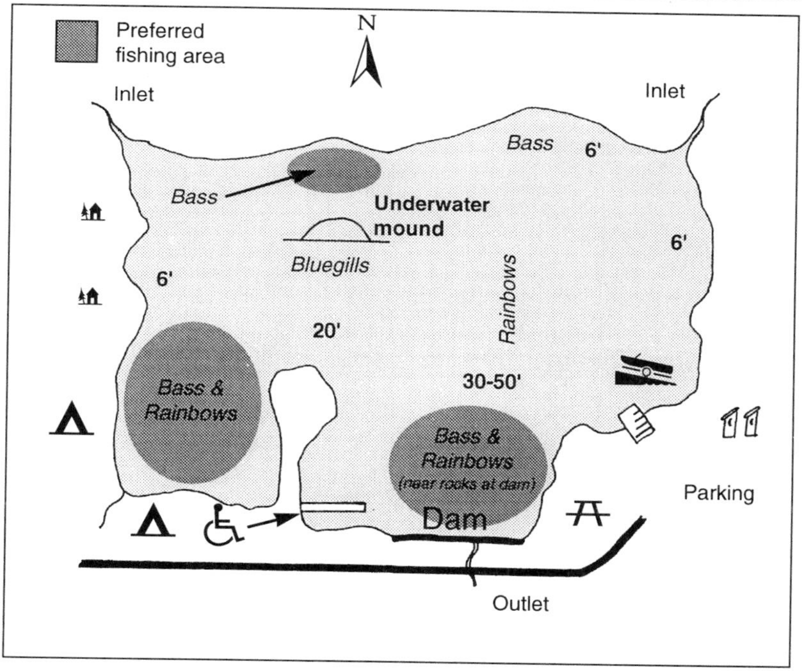

Preferred fishing area

N

Inlet

Inlet

Bass   6'

Bass

Underwater mound

Bluegills

Rainbows

6'

6'

20'

Bass & Rainbows

30-50'

Bass & Rainbows
(near rocks at dam)

Parking

Dam

Outlet

Spring, summer or fall this is the lake that has it all! At an elevation of about 1,400 feet it is only 45 minutes away from Sandy, Oregon and the road is asphalt all the way. To reach the lake take Highway 26 east from Sandy to Highway 35. Follow 35 about four miles to the White River Recreational Area. The large parking area on the right is where you turn right to get on the White River Road and Road 48. Drive on Road 48 for about 22 miles until you see a sign for the Sportsman Park. Turn left at the Sportsman Park sign and turn right at the next road. You will be at the campground sign.

You may turn left into the campground or go straight ahead to the dam and the day use area. The day use area has outhouses, a picnic area and a primitive boat launch site. As you fish the lake throughout the summer you will notice that the boat launch site becomes somewhat unusable as the lake water recedes, leaving a squishy mud shore. No boat motors are allowed on this lake.

The campground and restrooms are kept clean. If you don't like noise go camping in early spring or late fall when the kids are in school. If you park in the campground be prepared to pay a fee even though you may not be camping overnight. We avoid a parking fee by parking at the day use area just before crossing the dam. We enter the water near the dam and then paddle around the lake to where we are going to fish for the day.

Every year that we have fished here Oregon Fish and Wildlife has stocked this lake with brooders as well as small stocker rainbows. With brooders and holdovers you can catch up to 10-pound rainbows here. The lake also has a good population of largemouth bass and some bluegills. We have seen some monster bass at Rock Creek. Even though most of the bluegills we have caught are fairly small we have also caught some large ones.

For anyone who cares to know the bank fishermen use worms, Garlic Power Bait and eggs. They are a successful group of fishermen most of the time. The boaters row around pulling spinners, Hot Shots and Flatfish behind their boats and everyone is usually catching fish.

In the spring when the lake is full of water it is about 140 acres. This time of year we find the best fishing around the campground side of the lake. There is a small feeder stream coming into the lake and a lot of cover in which the fish can hide as they search for food or prepare to spawn. For spring fishing use a floating line with 16 feet of leader and a size 10 green lightly weighted Woolly Bugger or brown

Woolly Worm lightly weighted (no tail).

This time of year the fish can't decide whether they want food near the top or on the bottom of the lake. We catch more fish near the surface of the water but we also catch them on size 6 black or brown Woolly Buggers, weighted. In the afternoon when the fish start actively surface feeding in the shallow water, tie on a size 14 or 16 gray Soft Hackle, olive Gold-Ribbed Hare's Ear or a Pheasant Tail Nymph with a gold rib. Cast at rings, strip short small strips and pause. The fish take the flies subsurface.

In the summer we use size 8 brown Woolly Buggers or size 10 Zug Bugs for the trout and size 10 green Woolly Buggers and minnow patterns for bass. Use the green Woolly Bugger if damselflies are hatching near shore areas. We have caught bass and trout on tan Dry Caddis and Damselflies. Plop them down next to a bush or weeds where the fish are feeding and wait for the happening.

There is another excellent area across the lake on the far side which also has a feeder stream coming into it. It is much farther for our foot motors to take us, so we fish the easier access water. We use floating lines with 10 feet of leader for most areas near and around the shore. At the dam and in the deeper channels near the center of the lake use intermediate sinking lines.

Since the lake is used for irrigation, by late summer and fall the water level drops quickly and the lake may only hold five or 10 acres of water. All of the fish are forced to migrate to the dam. You can see almost all of the stumps in the lake this time of year. The first time we saw the lake in the fall we couldn't believe what we saw. Standing on the dam and looking to the left on the far side of the lake channel there is a hump sticking up near the top of the water. This is the area where we find many bluegills all summer. Use size 10-12 olive Soft Hackles and Gold-Ribbed Hare's Ears to catch the fish. This lake also has chironomids hatching during the day and you will need to match the colors to catch fish on them.

In the fall Rock Creek Reservoir is a favorite place for us to stop on our way to somewhere else. Cast from the bank when the reservoir is low. A size 8 or 10 small brown Woolly Bugger should work. We always practice catch and release but it is especially important in the fall at this reservoir because the fish do not stand much of a chance with the water at such a low level. Have your fun and release the fish unharmed. I imagine the fish would taste muddy if you tried to eat them anyway. We have a lot of fun this time of year. You will too as you catch the large fish and release them, knowing that they will probably live through the winter and be waiting for you to catch them again in the spring. Don't forget to try mud fishin' here, I have caught some big bass using the mud method!

A funny thing happened on this lake which should serve as a reminder for you to stay in your tube if you are not familiar with bank areas. One day we felt energetic and paddled over to the far side of the lake. The wind came up and the fish quit biting. I let the wind blow me down to the other end of the lake. Jim yelled at me, saying he had found what the fish were hitting so I decided to get out of the lake and walk back to where Jim was catching fish. I figured it would be easier to walk than kick against the wind for a quarter of a mile.

I must have chosen to get out of the lake at the only place around the whole lake that wasn't soft mud. As I was walking I noticed that I had to walk farther away from the water to stay on solid ground. Reaching a spot where I thought I could enter the water I found mud, mud and more mud. I picked up some sticks and rocks and tried to make a trail to the water. It worked until I put my fins on and stepped into the water away from my rock and stick trail. My fins totally disappeared under the mud. I was forced to plop down into my tube with my feet buried beneath me. What a dilemma! I had to dig out my fins with my hands and wound up with mud everywhere. If I put any pressure on my fins to push me out into deeper water I was stuck again. If I pulled too hard with my legs it felt as if I was going to pull my fins and boots off. At one point I almost tipped my tube over. I'm sure I looked like a Mud Duck scrounging for a meal.

After I was finally free I had mud on my face, hat, hair, globs on my rod and reel and my float tube was a nasty gooey brown mess. The worst part of this story was that by the time I had gotten unstuck and paddled over to Jim the hot fly had frozen over.

Round Lake

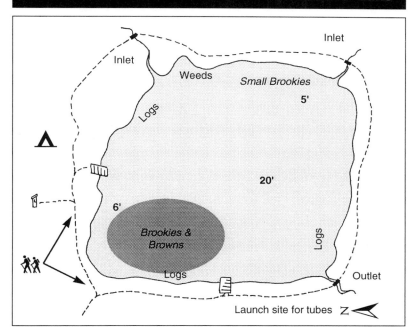

*T*o reach Round Lake follow 224 east out of Estacada, Oregon until you see the sign for Road 46. Take Road 46 to the Road 63 sign. Follow Road 63 past the Collawash River. This road will turn into Forest Service Road 6370. Be aware that log trucks use this road. The gravel road will lead you right to the parking area which is about a quarter-mile hike from the lake. The lake is an hour and 15 minute drive from Estacada.

Don't be surprised if you encounter deer, bear, grouse or even a cougar on this road. The drive to Round Lake will be worth every particle of dust you inhale. The lake has brookies up to 15 inches and browns up to eight pounds with an average length of 16 to 19 inches. The maximum depth of Round Lake is 20 feet. Basically we fish the northeast end of the lake where the water is three to eight feet deep over submerged weeds.

We were driving up to the lake one drizzly gray afternoon and saw something in the road ahead of us. We continued our approach; the animal didn't move. We got to about 20 yards and could plainly see we were looking at a cougar. The animal must have weighed over 90 pounds. It was soaking wet and the tail was long. The tail was as long as the cat. The size of the cougar, including the tail, was over half of the width of road. It watched us as we stopped the truck. We all looked at each other and then the cat jumped into the air, turning his body around 180 degrees in one leap. One more bound took him into the forest. This cat was as big or bigger than any cat I have seen at the zoo. We figured he had been dining on a lot of deer to grow to this size.

Bait fishing is prohibited at Round Lake (1992 regulations). Flies and lures must have barbless hooks. If you don't know when or what fly to fish you will probably leave Round Lake grumbling to yourself that there aren't any fish in the water. Then on your unhappy quarter-mile hike out you bump into us and we tell you that the fish here bite on every cast! We see you smile to yourself, secretly acknowledging that we are the biggest liars you have ever run into. What the heck? You spent all of that time driving here—why not follow these folks in and watch them for a while?

Walking back to the lake Jim goes into his dissertation about the three distinct emerging periods the *Callibaetis* mayfly goes through during the spring and summer months. From mid-April through May, depending on the water temperature, the *Callibaetis* start hatching around 9:00 to 10:00 a.m. hatching until noon. In the first part of June the hatch may start around 1:00 p.m. and in August the hatch won't start until 4:00 or 5:00 p.m. and can keep going into the night, depending on the water temperature. His explanation has taken us to the edge of the lake where we have launched our tubes.

Paddling out from the shore, we notice the first *Callibaetis* struggling to be free of its shuck on top of the water. We stop to watch this minor miracle of nature. A squirming body is suddenly free from the underwater world of lake weeds that he has called home for weeks, months or maybe years. Shedding his nymphal shuck, the tiny transparent wings unfold and flutter. Wings flash and dry in seconds in the sunlight. He bobs up and down across the surface of the water while attempting to release his small gray body from the grip of surface film. With each attempt at flight his long delicate white forked tails dip into the water, leaving a tell tale sign of his journey across the water.

At last he is strong enough to fly and mate within the swarm, fulfilling his life cycle. It isn't long until the weeds along the shore are harboring the females who lay hundreds of eggs. The swarm is as thick as a heavy snowstorm in the middle of winter—thousands of them. The guy on the bank yells, "Let me get a dry fly!" For some reason the big fish prefer the *Callibaetis* nymph. If you want to catch small brookies be our guest and cast a dry fly. We hope you can keep track of it!

Hold on: here comes Jaws! If you are quiet you will hear him slurping and sucking up great gobs of nymphs just under and on the surface of the water over the weedbeds. He sounds as if he really appreciates a good meal. Have your rod ready! Use a floating line with either one, two or three weighted *Callibaetis* nymphs. The idea is to have enough weight to get the fly down to the weeds. The leader must be long enough to allow you to fish right on top of or in the weeds. This is where we start the action. Strip this fly in slowly. In nature these tiny flies don't leap tall buildings.

This is important information that will enable you to catch fish at Round Lake. When you cast your line any distance away from you, watch where the line touches the water at the closest point to your rod tip. Don't try to watch your line where the fly has entered the water. You will not be able to see the subtle movement of your line from a distance. When you strip slowly and the line jumps it will be a brookie. If the line stops it will be a brown. As soon as the line jumps or stops, set the hook. If you wait to feel the fish take the fly it will probably be too late to hook the fish. Remember to watch the line where it touches the water off your rod tip.

If you arrive at the lake between hatches when nothing is going on your best bet is to grab an intermediate sinking line and head for deeper water. Tie a size 10 brown or green Woolly Bugger on the bottom of your leader with a black Chironomid and a Scud Fly as droppers.

This is a beautiful place to camp: tables, nice tent sites, outhouses and a trail around the small lake. Round Lake is a perfect place to catch fish. Don't carry any type of heavy boat into this lake. Jim did this with a friend of his who didn't own a float tube. Jim was no longer a friend by the time they hiked back to the car.

Please practice catch and release. It takes years for the fish to grow to the size that you want to be catching. Take your camera and snap a picture and then carefully allow the fish to return to his home alive and healthy so he can entertain the rest of us. We need to take responsibility for our lakes and protect the fish. If you need to catch fish and eat them, only keep stocker trout. A big dead fish is nothing to brag about. Show your friends a picture of a giant fish and be proud that you released him to grow even bigger. Our respect is limited for people who feel they need to kill big browns. We have told you how to catch them so you can have fun catching, not killing. We will tell you where to go to catch a steelhead from your float tube on your fly rod if you want to eat a big fish! Look for this information under the last lake in this book—which really isn't a lake at all!

Timothy Lake

*T*imothy is a large lake that sits at an elevation of 3,200 feet. It covers about 1,440 acres. On the south side of the lake there are beautiful campgrounds with outhouses and boat ramps for launching boats. Because of the size of this lake and the fact that we have two fins on our feet for motors, we will break the lake up into a couple of sections where we feel fish are plentiful.

From Estacada, Oregon take highway 224 east past the Ripplebrook Campground. After crossing the bridge just past the campground, turn left on Road 57 which is signed for Timothy Lake. Take Road 57 7.3 miles until you reach the intersection of 57 and 58. (Road 58 is an asphalt road. Road 57 is gravel but shorter and was closed all of 1992.) Turn left onto Road 58. This road will intersect Forest Service Road 5810 after traveling approximately one mile. Turn right on 5810. Stay on 5810 for 7.5 miles. Turn right or left at the intersection of 5810 and 5890 depending on where you plan to fish.

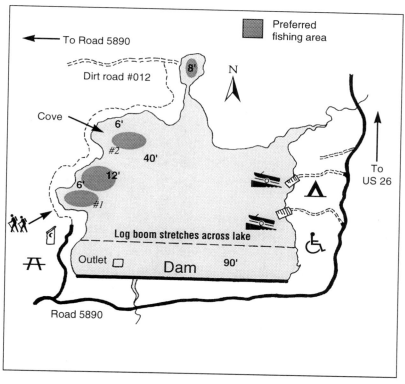

To Road 5890

Preferred fishing area

Dirt road #012

N

Cove

6'

#2

40'

12'

6'

#1

Log boom stretches across lake

Outlet

Dam

90'

Road 5890

To US 26

If you wish to fish the northeast end of the lake channel, turn left at the intersection and drive until you run out of asphalt. At the end of the asphalt continue driving on the gravel road for 3.8 miles and then turn right onto a dirt road. It is signed 5890 with 012 as smaller numbers. The dirt road will take you to the lake in half a mile. There is a primitive camping area here. This will be our second fishing area.

To fish the first of our two areas, turn right at the main intersection. Just before you cross the dam, turn left following the day use area signs. At the end of this road park at the beginning of the hiking trail that goes around the lake. The day use fishing area on the north side of the lake has float tube launch sites along the shoreline. There is one site suitable to launch a light boat if you care to drag it into the lake over fine gravel and sand. This side of the lake does not have a boat ramp but you can launch your float tube almost anywhere. Watch for stumps and rocks when launching. Occasionally we hike from the beginning of the hiking trail about a quarter of a mile before we launch. Other times we launch right below the beginning of the hiking trail and do a little more paddling and fishing. The beauty of this area is that you can launch anywhere and have access to good fishing.

Paddling away from shore, head north paralleling the shore. We think it is around a mile or less to the cove at the far end of this section of the lake. This we will refer to as No. 1 shore. The cove on this end of the lake is sometimes protected from the wind.

The wind changes directions frequently on the lake. Many days we have started out with the wind pushing us across the lake to our destination, making our task easy and then have it change directions in the afternoon to give us a free ride back to where we had started in the morning. Of course it can work against you, too. We catch fish all over this large area. You will find many days when you will be able to fish without a hint of wind as the early morning sun takes the chill out of the air.

Shore No. 1 is about six feet deep. Twenty feet from the bank you can see the tree stumps under the water. Then it drops to 12 feet deep 30 feet from shore in most places and then to 15 to 20 feet and on to out to over 40 feet quite rapidly. When you are about half or three-quarters of the way down Shore No. 1 you can cut across the lake and be in front of Shore No. 2 or you can fish down to the cove and then cut across the cove and continue around the shoreline to No. 2.

At the end of the cove and facing the cove you will see another point coming out into the lake and more straight shoreline to your right. This will be Shore No. 2. If you cut across the lake before going to the cove you will be going over some mighty deep water. You would need to change to a sinking line in the deeper water. The water will be over 40 feet deep but eventually you will wind up about 100 yards off the shoreline of No. 2 in about 12 to 16 feet of water. About 50 yards off Shore No. 2 you will find five to 14 feet of water. The stumps will be very visible. Shore No. 2 is very long and fishing is good in six feet of water as well as the water 14 feet deep. Shore No. 2 generally has more fishing boats cruising the area. We troll slowly fishing these areas.

In the spring we find Shore No. 2 most productive. We tie on 14-16 feet of six-pound test fishing leader. You must have strong leader as the large fish can break off. Using a floating line, tie a large brown Woolly Bugger on as the end fly. The fish will usually hit the Woolly Bugger due to the crawdad population in this lake. There are even commercial crawfish boats on the lake. If there are no visible signs of hatches a size 10-12 Pheasant Tail Nymph, size 12 brown Gold-Ribbed Hare's Ear or a Cate's Turkey with the gray legs and tail cut off will usually get good results. Fish the nymphs in the appropriate manner with small strips and many pauses and try a twitch if the strips don't work. Also try a Bucktail Coachman or size 10 Spruce Fly stripped long and slowly.

In the summer start off by using size 4-8 green or brown weighted Woolly Buggers or weighted green Gold-Ribbed Hare's Ear (size 8). A dropper fly size 12 orange Tied-Down Caddis (best in June after the water is warmer)or a size 14 Gold-Ribbed Hare's Ear, a size 14 Gray-Ribbed Hare's Ear, or a size 12 or 14 black Chironomid with white head. Look for cases on the water before putting the Chironomid on. This lake is full of chironomids.

Depending on how warm the weather is in June or July the fish consume many dragonfly nymphs. Some days it takes forever to get down to the cove on Shore No. 1 using the green Gold-Ribbed Hare's Ear (size 8 or 6) or size 8 green Woolly Buggers. What a great problem to have! In the month of June or July use a size 10 or 12 Iron Blue Wingless. In mid June or July there are hatches of size 14-16 olive to medium green scuds. The fish gorge themselves for a few days and then the green scuds seem to lose their fish appeal.

July usually sports an abundant hatch of small chironomids on Shore No. 2 in early to mid morning. Later in the day your end fly should be a size 8 green Gold-Ribbed Hare's Ear or a size 8 green cased, brown winged Caddis Nymph. As summer progresses the fish seem less interested in the dragonfly nymphs but will still hit them occasionally. July and August can be a good month for gray Gold-Ribbed Hare's Ears. Tan Gold-Ribbed Hares Ears (size 14) and brown Woolly Buggers (size 4) should still work.

In the month of July on Shore No. 1 near the hiking trail head in the early evening there is often a fairly decent *Callibaetis* hatch. Tie on a size 14 or 16 *Callibaetis,* toss it out and be patient. Let the fly sit quietly for a few seconds and pull in long, slow strips, pause, repeat and watch for your line to jump or be jerked out of your hands. We have also noted *Callibaetis* hatching down at the cove next to the banks. Some of these hatches are not very predictable. We have also seen *Hexagenia* hatch on this lake. Not having the proper imitation I use a size 6 Matt's Fur. The fish hit this fly hard.

You are going to catch many small bright kokanee, stocker and holdover rainbows, cutthroat and brook trout. We have caught fish as large as five pounds. You can catch fish all day long if you follow the hatches around the lake. Keep an eye on the birds, noting when they group together in a certain spot on the lake, dipping into surface of the water. Note the time of day and remember the area. The birds will give you an instant message that there is a hatch going on. If you can't paddle to that spot in time to see what is hatching and the birds spend a lot of time there make sure you are in that area at the same time the next day. This information has helped us more times than we can count. Fishing at Timothy Lake can be slow as the weather cools. Your best bet would be to switch to minnow patterns. Don't be surprised when the kokanee jump on the minnows. The fly is almost as big as the fish.

To reach our second fishing area in the northeast corner of the lake at the end of the channel, drive back down the road to the intersection we talked about earlier and follow the directions. You will be fishing a shallow area of water from four to six feet deep over and around weedbeds. Launch any place along the shore avoiding stumps and large rocks. In the summer all you will have to do is to try to match the hatch and then fish your nymphs. We use floating lines with slightly weighted flies and about 10 feet of leader. Use size 10 green Soft Hackles, size 16 *Callibaetis* Nymphs, size 12 Gold-Ribbed Hare's Ears and size 8 green body, tan wing Caddis Emergers.

This section of the lake has an excellent damsel and dragonfly hatch. The hatch seems to take place off and on beginning in late morning and lasting into late afternoon. It is not uncommon to see large fish slurping up spent dragonflies close to the shore. At this fishing location our fishing position is stationary once we reach our destination on the water. In the summer we paddle 25 to 50 yards off shore and cast toward rising fish or to the outer edges of the protruding water weeds. The retrieve is three or four quick inch-long strips and then a pause. Do not pause long enough for the fly to settle too far into the weeds. Watch for your line to jump and set the hook. After two or three minutes give the fly a little twitch and let it sit quietly once again. When fishing Woolly Buggers retrieve in large 12-inch sharp pulls and pause for five seconds before sharply pulling again.

We have been on this lake when the water was almost as rough as the ocean and when it was as smooth as glass. Head for the bank when it becomes too windy. The trail goes around most of the lake and it will be easier to hike out than paddle out if the wind doesn't let up. We take a lunch break when the wind comes up. Often the wind will stop blowing after 10 to 20 minutes and the lake will become calm again.

This lake is my favorite. I hope you enjoy fishing here as much as I do. Before I learned how to catch fish at this lake I spent many hours without seeing a single insect hatch anywhere. I had gone through boxes of flies and spools of leader with one small trout to show for my efforts. Growing weary from days of effort I leaned back in my tube to enjoy the cold gray sky and saw an osprey sitting in a tree. I watched as he flew out over the water and began his circular search. It didn't take long until he swooped down and flew back into the sky with his catch. His effortless skill turned me green with envy. Then with the dangling fish still wiggling and dripping water onto the surface of the lake he circled around me 50 feet above my head. I'll assure you that this is low for an osprey with a float tuber sitting under him. Maybe he didn't think I was alive since I hadn't caught more than one fish all day. I interpreted his actions as insults. What a sadistic bird! He flaunted his catch for five minutes. I have seen many birds catch fish and eat them but this bird was truly weird. His actions were the straw that broke the camel's back. Having had enough discouragement for one day I headed for my car. I will never forget the strange osprey but I accepted his actions as a challenge while I mentally prepared a list of new flies to try the next day.

Trillium Lake

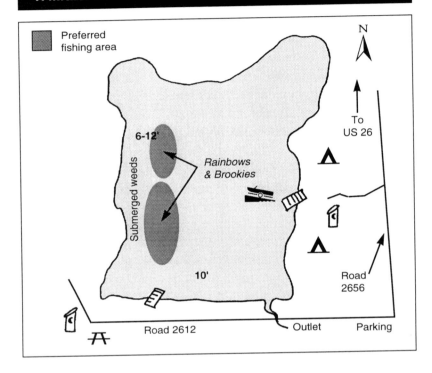

Preferred fishing area

6-12'

Submerged weeds

Rainbows & Brookies

10'

N

To US 26

Road 2656

Road 2612

Outlet

Parking

*T*rillium Lake is easy to find. It is a short 25-mile trip from Sandy, Oregon. From Sandy, stay on Highway 26 past Government Camp. Continue driving on until you see Snow Bunny on the left side of the highway. Just past Snow Bunny there will be a sign on the right side of the road for Trillium Lake. Turn right on Forest Service Road 2656. The road goes around the lake turning into Forest Service Road 2612. Park and launch at the far southwest end of the lake. You will find outhouses and a large parking area. You can launch carefully from the rock bank where the bait fishermen fish. Not the best launch site but we have launched from worse.

If you have any out-of-state relatives coming to visit be sure to drive them to Trillium Lake for a photograph. This is probably one of the most photographed views of Mt. Hood. Notice the groomed glacier fields on which you can ski all summer if you aren't fishing. On a clear sunny day the view is indeed breathtaking. Facing beautiful Mount Hood from where you launch you will be looking over 60 acres of water. The deepest water is about 20 feet. See all of the fine lily pads on your left? This is where we start fishing along the east side of the bank. We will keep about 40 to 60 feet off shore casting near the weeds using floating line with 10 feet of four- to six-pound leader.

This lake has a fine *Callibaetis* hatch. When the bugs start hatching we fish a size 16 *Callibaetis* Nymph. We also catch rainbow trout on slightly weighted size 8 black Woolly Buggers, size 12 Gold-Ribbed Hare's Ears, size 16 Dry Peacock Herl Midges, size 12 Adams dries and size 12 Mosquito dries. The rainbow trout are from nine to 13 inches and are a lot of fun to catch. The retrieve is slow long pulls for the *Callibaetis* Nymph. The size 8 black Woolly Bugger will need to be fished on the lake bottom with three or four six- to eight-inch fast pulls and then allowing it to settle back down to the bottom of the lake. Pause a few seconds before starting the retrieve again.

At this lake you can cast dry flies to rising fish and experience great success. After casting a dry fly let it sit quietly for a few seconds before twitching the line. This should attract the attention of the fish.

A good point in favor of this lake is that it is not far from Portland and is heavily stocked. You catch rainbows and brookies. The campground is very clean and well maintained; there are restrooms and a boat ramp at the campground. This is a peaceful lake as there are no boat motors allowed. This would be a good lake to teach the kids or grandchildren to fly fish from a float tube or rubber raft. When time is limited make a quick trip to Trillium and fish in the early evenings when the fish are feeding around the lily pads.

I am very fortunate to have a couple of grown children who will fish with me when they have the time. My son John was fishing with Jim and me and we were watching John's efforts to cast a fly. He was a novice caster but was really getting into casting. He was getting out a great amount of line for a beginner. I suggested that he would be safer if he would quit whipping around so much line. He choose to ignore the advice so Jim and I moved our tubes a safe distance from his fly.

About 20 minutes later John came paddling over to me. He got real close, bumping my tube. Next he reached up, stretching the line from the fly stuck in his neck making the fly protrude. Then he said, "Mom, Frankenstein is more than a little embarrassed and has a small problem!" His sense of humor has always been one of his greatest assets. I asked Jim to inflict the pain of fly removal. After Jim removed the fly, John wanted to know if the five-inch hole in his neck was spurting blood. We assured him that we couldn't even see where the fly had pierced the skin.

John has since learned to cast and can catch more than his fair share of fish on a fly rod. He still fishes with me even after I tell this story! The fact of the matter is that almost every fly fisherman has hooked himself more than once and will probably continue to do so as long as he fishes with flies. At one lake I saw two people fly fishing on the bank next to each other. A small gust of wind came up just as one of the guys cast his fly. The fly wound up in the seat of his friend's pants. Cover up, wear glasses and keep on fishing—that's our motto.

Walter Wirth Pond

*I*n February, March and April, if the weather is slightly warmer than usual and cabin fever is ruining your happy disposition it is time for a fishing fix. Grab your long underwear and join us at Walter Wirth Pond near Salem, Oregon. When you go fishing at this lake we guarantee it will not be because it is a quiet, isolated, serene or remote fishing location. It will be because we are all frantically desperate to catch fish in a lake after being house bound all winter!

The pond is located just off Interstate 5. From Portland, Oregon head south toward Salem. Just past Salem take the turnoff for Highway 22. At the top of the ramp turn right and get into the left lane. Go to the second traffic light and turn left. After turning left there is a stop sign. Turn left again. It is only a short distance until you make another left turn into the park. The park road will take you right to the pond.

Install earplugs after you park your car. You may launch tubes

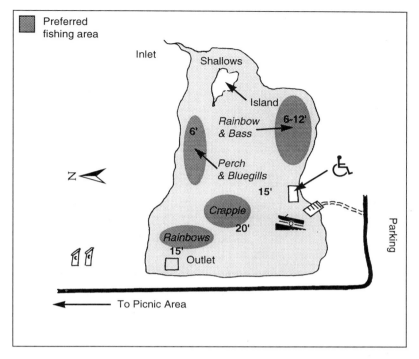

from any location and there is a primitive small boat ramp. The pond is sandwiched between the I-5 freeway and an airport. It also has a hefty hatch of bank fishing people, barking dogs, rafts, sailboards, crying babies, canoes and other desperate float tubers like yourself. Ah yes. . . we will also mention that it is full of fish. This is a year-round fishery. We think the pond must be stocked monthly throughout the winter with brooder rainbows and some brooder brookies. If you add two- to four-pound brooders to the existing bass, bluegill, crappie and perch fishery we guarantee it spells spring fishing fun!

Depending on the kind of winter we had you may be able to sit in the water as early as February. We prefer to wait until the water warms and the hatches start and usually begin fishing in late March if our sour attitudes allow us to wait that long. Again depending on how cold the winter has been April and May are usually good fishing months. If winter has been very cold and the temperature doesn't warm up by April and May then the best fishing months may be May and June. In 1993 we had a long, cool spring and summer. It didn't warm up until late July. This made the water in all of the lakes stay colder for a longer period of time and the hatches were not as good.

Walter Wirth is a fairly shallow pond with a depth of about 20 feet in the center. The lake is usually off color and the average depth is approximately six to 12 feet 20 feet off shore. We have found most of the crappie in the center of the lake fishing an intermediate sinking lines using size 12 black Woolly Buggers. Jim has a special fly for a species of chironomid that hatches in this pond. The chironomid he ties is on a size 10-12 hook and has a yellow butt, olive top and white ostrich herl gills. All fish will hit this chironomid when it is hatching. We also catch fish on size 8 olive or black Woolly Buggers.

When the water temperature reaches about 60 degrees you can catch bass and bluegills around spawning beds near the banks in the weeds. Try any size 12 dry fly or a streamer. Be sure to stay out of the casting range of bank fishermen. The bank fishermen fish a bobber and fly and catch many fish with this technique as well as using the old standby, worms. The flies seem to be size 10-12 and are white. We fish a light-colored mayfly or tan caddis subsurface on floating lines with similar results when the fish aren't hitting anything on or near the bottom of the lake.

We were fishing here on one occasion when a big brooder poked its head up out of the water and looked around. We couldn't believe what we had just witnessed. We were commenting on the fish's strange behavior when we saw the head come bobbing up out of the water for a second time. Its head had to be five inches above the surface. The fish did a slow pirouette in the water, pinpointing our position and looked us squarely in the eye before it slid beneath the surface and out of sight. We could honestly say we had never made eye contact with a fish before. It didn't take us long to figure out what the fish was doing. A brooder is fed pellets by humans and this one was obviously hungry. It had come up looking around to see if it was time for someone to feed it. It was a strange feeling having a fish watch you! Believe us when we tell you the fish didn't have to beg to be fed again.

No overnight camping is allowed. The restrooms are about an

eighth of a mile past the north end of the lake. Near the restrooms there are playgrounds and picnic areas along with another pond where no floating devices are allowed. It looks too brushy to fish with a fly rod from the bank but it could be a sleeper!

Walter Wirth will do when nothing else is available. While catching fish you begin to forget about the distractions. We feel that it is worth at least a few early spring and summer visits. If you live close to this lake and like fishing here be sure to fish in the summer as the fish are very willing feeders on wet as well as dry flies all around the bank areas.

Pools on the Clackamas

*J*im sat in his float tube protected from the hot rays of the summer sun by the narrow canyon walls. There was not another soul around and the only sound he could hear was the water rolling over the rocks at the head of the pool. He smiled to himself because he knew that the effort it had taken to hike down the hill an eighth of a mile or so would be well worth it. The fly line tightened. He set the hook with a quick upward motion and found himself connected to 10 pounds of jumping, shimmering steelhead. Mind and hands now work together as one; the arched rod bending as he and the fish engage in battle. There are no mistakes made in this fight: the fish simply tires out and must allow Jim to free the hook from the corner of its mouth.

Both are winners as Jim lets the heavy-bodied fish slip from has grasp and slide back into the water. The fish pauses long enough to thank Jim as only a fish can; with a grateful slap of his tail on the surface of the water. Laughingly Jim wipes the droplets of water from his face with a shirtsleeve while shaking a cramped hand in an effort to revive it. He can't help wondering if a coho will be the next victim of the Red Woolly Bugger dangling from the end of the line.

When would a river be as safe a place to fish from a float tube as a lake? Perhaps when the water flow is less than 50 cubic feet per hour. At this speed if you took a stick and threw it upstream 30 yards it would take about half an hour for the stick to drift back to you. Let us assure you that we are talking about very slowly moving water.

We know where there is just such a place for you to float tube providing you use common sense and do not attempt to launch your tube during or right after a major rainstorm. At this location you can spend many summer, fall and winter days hooking big fish to your hearts' content. The water depth at this prime location averages about 15 feet deep. You will find no boaters as boats cannot access this portion of the river. If you encounter a hardy bank fisherman you can simply paddle out of his line of reach and still have great water to fish in as there are about seven pools you can access as well as the long strip of narrow canyon.

Here are some facts we think you will find interesting. In 1992, 6,000 summer steelhead, nearly 4,000 spring Chinook, a few fall Chinook and almost 4,000 coho salmon moved through this section of water. If this information doesn't make you want to grab your fishing rod and float tube and head for the Clackamas River then you should have someone nearby to check your pulse and see if you are still alive!

This fishing hole is located in front of Faraday Lake about a mile east of Estacada and only 40 miles from Portland. Outside of Estacada, turn right at the sign for Faraday Lake and drive down into the parking lot. You are not allowed to drive onto the bridge. Park and walk out onto the bridge and have a look down into the river. Note the pools you can see from your vantage point and look for fish swimming in them. Check to see if any fish are rising or rolling. If you see any indications that the fish are here hike across the bridge and turn right, walking down the road toward the river. Launch above the rapids as close to the bridge as possible. It is easy for you to kick back up to the bridge because the water is moving so slowly. This narrow canyon with its pools will be your fishing hole.

During the months of May, June and July you will be catching more steelhead than anything else. They are at a depth of about four to six feet in the pools. You will need to use a floating line and retrieve your fly very slowly. The fly should be an unweighted Woolly Bugger tied on a Mustad 9672 size 4 hook. The most productive colors will be black, brown, olive, red, purple and pink.

When the spring Chinook come into the river around late June, July and August you can fish for and keep any salmon you catch. After August 15 you are not allowed to keep salmon but you can still keep steelhead if you want to. The salmon prefer the deeper water in the pools. Normally you will not be able to see them from the bridge. If they are in the river they will be on the bottom in the deep water. They often chase the steelhead out of any pool they wish to occupy.

In order to catch them you will need to put on a heavy sinking line such as a Wet Cel III. The majority of the salmon will not hit hard. If you think you are snagged, set the hook. If it is a rock it will still be a rock but if it is a fish you will have no regrets. You can catch the salmon on an Olive Matuka but they have also hit pink or red Woolly Buggers weighted and presented deep.

Jim sat in his tube one day for 1 1/2 hours with the rod butt digging hard into his stomach while the tip of the rod was under water. He had to wait this long to get rid of the huge salmon he had on. It pulled him around the water in his tube. He said his arms were killing him from the strain of just trying to hold on to the rod. These fish do not run out of power quickly.

In the fall the first run of coho come into these pools around the end of September or early October. These fish are supposed to go the hatchery on Eagle Creek but many of the fish find Eagle Creek too low and warm so they bypass the creek and move on up the Clackamas. These coho definitely prefer purple or pink Woolly Buggers. When you hook a coho you are going to know what it is like to try to hang onto the tail of a race horse doing 30 miles an hour. This fish has it all—he is an Olympic Gold Medalist. He can jump higher, run faster, power dive and fight harder than any steelhead. The good news is that he is a sprinter and is all pooped out after about 10 minutes, so you can release him, hook another and start all over again.

In mid-November a run of winter coho comes into the pools. Now both summer steelhead and coho are available. Both species will take the same fly. You won't know which fish you have hooked until it shakes its head (coho) or takes off like a bullet (steelhead). The winter coho normally hit best from daylight until 9:30 a.m. The winter steelhead do not show up in these pools until mid-December. They will often hit flies all day.

After having a slow fishing day one winter Jim decided that he needed to tie Woolly Buggers with more flash to represent a minnow. He knew that minnows were about the only thing moving around in the pools other than the big fish this time of year. He experimented by tying Woolly Buggers with Krystal Flash trying to make them look a little more like minnows. The new Woolly Buggers were not very effective but they were a step in the right direction. They are two winner flies. The first has a royal blue braided mylar body with a inch-long royal blue marabou tail. It has a palmered royal blue saddle hackle. The second fly has a gold cactus tinsel body, inch-long bright yellow marabou tail and palmered yellow dyed grizzly hackle. Both of these flies are tied on the mustad 9672 size 4 hooks.

You can catch fish out of these pools many months of the year. The water in the pools will rarely change. In July P.G.E. increases the water flow to help the Chinook move on upriver to spawn. They usually shut the water flow down by 10:00 a.m. When the water flow shuts down the big fish can't figure out what has happened to all of the water and zip around the pools like crazy. They must be agitated because they go on the bite after this happens. Other than P.G.E. fooling around with the water level the only other times you won't want to float tube at this location will be a few days out of the year when we are having a torrential rainy season and the water is at or near flood stage. Under normal conditions you will be able to float tube safely and on a good day catch all of the big fish you could ever want, fulfilling your wildest fishing dream. If you find out that this fishing area is to your liking and you don't live close consider staying in a motel in Estacada or camping at a campground. There are beautiful campgrounds on the upper Clackamas River and they are open from May to September.

New 1994 fishing regulations have closed these pools from November 1st through late April. The closure is to protect the wild winter coho from being harassed.

So now the best fishing in these pools will be from mid-June through October.

Lakes of the Mount Hood National Forest

Cold Water Game Fish Abbreviations

Br = Brown trout
Bt = Brook trout
Ct = Cutthroat trout
K = Kokanee
Rb = Rainbow trout
St = Steelhead

Name	Map Location	Elevation (ft)	Acreage	Depth (ft)	Fish
Anvil	T5S R8E S17	4000	2	5	Ct
Averill	T9S R8E S04	4650	12	11	Bt, Rb
Badger	T3S R10E S20	4500	35	33	Bt, Rb
Bear	T2N R9E S18	3800	2	12	Bt
Beth	T8S R6E S08	4450	5	35	Bt
Big Slide	T8S R6E S09	4250	4	10	Bt
Big Slide Upper	T8S R6E S10	4300	1	11	Bt
Black	T2N R8E S36	3800	4	5	Bt
Boulder big	T4S R10E S05	4600	11	17	Bt
Boulder little	T4S R10E S04	4800	6	5	Bt
Breitenbush	T9S R8E S25	5500	60	30	Bt
Brook	T8S R8-1/2E S26	4700	5	8	Bt
Buck	T5S R8E S30	4000	9	26	Bt
Bump	T8S R8E S28	4300	3	4	Bt
Burnt	T2S R8E S34	4100	8	25	Bt
Cast	T2S R8E S33	4450	7	17	Bt
Catalpa	T4S R9E S14	4100	3	8	Bt
Cigar	T9S R8E S10	5100	5	8	Bt
Clackamas	T5S R8E S35	3350	2	4	Bt, Rb, Ct
Clear	T4S R9E S30	3500	557	26	Bt, Rb
Clear	T5S R4E S14	3850	3	7	Bt, Ct
Collins	T3S R8E S24	3700	1	6	Bt, Rb
Cottonwood Mdws	T5S R7E S28	4050	6	4	Bt
Cripple Creek	T5S R7E S19	4300	15	4	Bt
Davey	T9S R8E S27	5200	2	14	Ct
Devils Meadow	T3S R8E S04	4100	2	7	Bt
Dinger	T5S R8E S09	4000	15	4	Bt, Ct
Double Peak	T9S R8E S09	4700	4	13	Bt, Rb
Dublin	T1N R7E S02	3500	2	9	Bt
Dumbbell	T2S R8E S32	4150	2	5	Rb, Ct
Ercrama	T8S R6E S20	4450	2	15	Ct
Finley	T9S R8E S03	4950	2	12	Bt, Rb
First	T9S R8E S02	4950	3	19	Rb, Ct
Fish	T8S R8E S34	4400	24	67	Bt, Ct
Fish	T1N R8E S02	4000	2	5	Bt, Rb
Frazier	T5S R7E S09	4100	3	8	Bt, Rb, Ct
Frog	T4S R9E S17	4000	11	8	Rb
Gibson	T9S R8-1/2E S24	5800	6	14	Bt
Gifford	T9S R8E S03	4950	9	56	Rb
Gifford lower	T9S R8E S03	4940	2	19	Bt, Rb
Harriet	T6S R7E S04	2000	23	45	Bt, Rb, Br, Ct
Head	T9S R8E S02	4950	6	9	Ct
Hicks	T1N R8E S03	4400	2	6	Bt
Hidden	T3S R8E S12	4000	2	13	Bt

Cold Water Game Fish Abbreviations

Br = Brown trout   Ct = Cutthroat trout   Rb = Rainbow trout
Bt = Brook trout   K = Kokanee   St = Steelhead

Name	Map Location	Elevation (ft)	Acreage	Depth (ft)	Fish
Hideaway	T5S R7E S21	3800	12	30	Bt, Rb
High	T6S R6E S06	4450	3	11	Bt
Horseshoe	T9S R8E S24	5400	14	17	Bt, Rb
Jean	T3S R10E S17	4800	6	18	Bt
Jeni	T7S R4E S19	3840	2		Bt
Jude	T8S R8E S25	4550	2	14	Bt
Kingsley	T2N R9E S22	3100	48	30	Rb
Lawrance	T1S R9E S22	3000	104	92	Rb, Ct
Lenore	T8S R6E S10	4800	5	11	Bt
Long	T9S R8E S12	4650	16	24	Bt, Rb
Lost	T1S R8E S10	3100	290	167	Bt, Rb, K, Br
Lower	T9S R8E S02	4750	15	73	Bt, Rb
Mangriff	T9S R8E S13	5000	1	14	Bt
Memaloose	T5S R5E S31	4100	8	5	Bt
Mirror	T3S R8E S23	4050	8	15	Bt, Rb
Monon	T9S R8E S13	5000	91	39	Bt, Rb
Multipor	T3S R8E S24	3800	3	5	Bt
Nekbobets	T9S R8E S10	5250	3	10	Bt, Rb
Nippon	T9S R8E S02	5000	3	6	Bt
North Fork Res.	T4S R4E S12	665	331	115	Rb, St
North	T2N R8E S24	4000	6	8	Bt
Nup Te Pa	T9S R8E S13	5000	2	25	Bt
Olallie	T9S R8E S11	4900	240	48	Bt, Rb
Otter	T1N R8E S11	4000	2	8	Bt
Pansy	T8S R6E S18	4000	7	4	Bt
Plaza	T4S R7E S18	3650	5	10	Bt
Pyramid	T9S R8E S27	5000	5	9	Bt
Pyramid	T5S R7E S11	4000	4	5	Bt
Rainey	T2N R8E S25	4100	10	8	Bt
Red	T8S R8E S08	4550	6	7	Bt, Rb
Rimrock	T9S R8E S10	5150	3	14	Bt
Ripplebrook	T6S R6E S03	1500	2	8	Rb
Rock lower	T5S R7E S08	4100	9	13	Bt, Rb
Rock middle	T5S R7E S08	4350	15	34	Bt, Rb
Rock upper	T5S R7E S17	4400	3	22	Bt, Rb
Round	T8S R7E S17	3750	9	20	Bt, Rb, Br
Russ	T8S R8-1/2E S26	4700	5	8	Bt
Salmon	T4S R7E S16	3800	2	3	Bt
Scout	T1N R8E S14	4400	3	6	Bt
Serene	T5S R7E S07	4350	20	46	Bt, Rb
Sheep	T9S R8E S04	4800	4	9	Bt, Rb
Shellrock	T5S R7E S17	4200	20	8	Bt, Rb
Shining	T4S R6E S36	3950	12	24	Bt, Rb
Si	T8S R8E S33	4250	3	10	Bt, Rb
Silver King	T8S R5E S24	4100	4	7	Bt
Skookum	T6S R5E S35	3800	4	14	Bt
Spinning	T9S R8E S22	4900	3	8	Bt

Cold Water Game Fish Abbreviations

Br = Brown trout	Ct = Cutthroat trout	Rb = Rainbow trout
Bt = Brook trout	K = Kokanee	St = Steelhead

Name	Map Location	Elevation (ft)	Acreage	Depth (ft)	Fish
Spud big	T9S R8E S04	4900	2	13	Bt
Spud little	T9S R8E S04	4900	1	14	Bt
Squaw	T4S R6E S13	3550	7	5	Bt
Surprise #1	T5S R6E S27	1500	3	15	Bt
Surprise #2	T6S R5E S27	4050	5	4	Bt, Rb
Surprise #3	T8S R8E S34	4350	4	2	Ct
Suzi	T4S R7E S31	4240	2	7	Bt
Timber	T5S R6E S34	1500	12	15	Rb
Timber	T9S R8E S14	5300	10	18	Bt, Rb
Timothy Mdws Res	T5S R8E S23	3200	1440	90	Bt, Rb, Ct, K
Top	T9S R8E S10	5000	3	6	Bt
Trillium	T3S R8E S36	3600	60	20	Bt, Rb
Twin big	T4S R9E S09	4150	18	18	Bt
Twin little	T4S R9E S04	4250	11	4	Bt
Twin lower	T8S R6E S29	4100	15	40	Bt
Twin upper	T8S R6E S30	4150	15	50	Bt
Upper	T9S R8E S15	5150	8	14	Bt
Veda	T4S R8E S02	4400	3	14	Bt
View	T9S R8E S14	5250	7	10	Bt
Wahtum	T1N R8E S10	4000	57	177	Bt
Wall	T9S R8E S04	4800	5	12	Bt, Rb
Warren	T2N R9E S16	3750	5	8	Bt
Welcome	T8S R6E S15	4200	6	8	Bt
Wendy Mdws	T5S R8E S21	3550	2	3	Ct
West	T8S R6E S16	4300	4	4	Bt
Williams	T5S R4E S26	3750	4	4	Bt, Ct
Wind	T3S R8E S26	4700	3	3	Bt

Maps are available from the following sources:

Distribution Section
Geological Survey
Federal Center
Denver, CO 80225

U.S. Forest Service
P.O. Box 3623 (319 S.W. Pine)
Portland, OR 97208

Bureau of Land Management
Oregon State Office
P.O. Box 2965 (729 N.E. Oregon Street)
Portland, OR 97208

Oregon State Forestry Department
Mapping Section
2600 State Street
Salem, OR 97310

Map Distribution Unit
Room 28
State Highway Building
Salem, OR 97310

Some maps are free. Others have a small charge. A number of maps prepared by private commercial companies are available at sporting good stores and other commercial outlets

Homeward Bound

While watching the evening sun slip into its nest just below the horizon I urgently call out to my brothers. They reply long before I see their slightly off centered V pattern darkly outlined against the red sky. I marvel at the skill and strength of my friends in flight, aware of how difficult it is to speak to each other and not give a side or downward glance; thus losing focus and order in the air. At last in loud discord and great disorder the geese descend to join me upon the water. Safe in their presence I now find comfort and reassurance and I'm no longer afraid of the songs of the coyote.

Dimly lit stars appear between scattered clouds while the breeze gently nudges us towards the shore. The combination of darkness and motion begin the stirrings of our evening desire to find rest and sleep. We go about the task of settling into the comfort and warmth our own bodies provide. Muted good nights float back and forth across the darkness as it envelops us. Tonight the request has come for me to stand guard. I diligently attempt to keep a watchful lookout for our enemies but tire quickly. The strength I had in my youth is almost forgotten as old age and an injured wing limits my daily search for food. My once strong neck grows weary and I seek comfort for my head beneath soft warm down while dreaming the dreams of the old.

I see endless miles of autumn sky and the continual honking of robust voices fills the air with messages urging the tired ones to keep up their exhausting pace. From these sounds we gain strength as our excitement builds. We sing our songs of life across the sky to the accompaniment of drumming wings whistling and beating rhythmically against the wind. The sounds inspire young and old alike to add their bit of history to this journey through perseverance. At last we reach the final destination of safe bountiful waterways and fields of golden grains for us to rest in and feast upon.

Abruptly I awaken! The warning is not in time and weary eyes do not see the slinking form approach. I am unaware until I feel the pressure of the coyote's jaws lock tightly around my body. Hundreds of my brothers' angry voices rise in chorus drowning out my feeble cries. Moments later the commotion subsides and I find peace with all that surrounds me. I see the remnants of my earthly existence pausing briefly upon the water: feathers, eager to be lifted by the great winds of tomorrow and carried effortlessly along the paths of my brothers forever.

—**Beverly M. Miller**

Jim and I were fishing at night in a lake in Washington. When the sun began to set the coyotes started to howl. The wild geese flew in to rest on the lake for the night and almost landed on top of us, mistaking us in our float tubes for islands. After darkness settled around us the quiet was suddenly shattered by the voices of hundreds of angry geese. I quickly surmised what had happened and started mentally writing this story.

Beverly's son, John Miller, at Barnes Butte Lake.

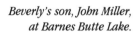

Doyle Goolsby at Nunley Lake in Washington.

Jim Bradbury showing off the brown trout he caught at Lanese Lake.

Beverly Miller and an early spring trout at Walter Wirth Pond.

Jim Bradbury at the very cold Lanese Lake.

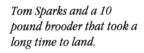

Tom Sparks and a 10 pound brooder that took a long time to land.

Beverly with a big catch, a rainbow at Rock Creek Reservoir.

Jim Bradbury with a brown trout at Round Lake.

Beverly takes her two grandsons, Guy and Lee Schoenborn, on their first float tube and fly fishing trip.

Jennifer and Christopher Miller with a 3 pound rainbow.

Fishing friend Edna exchanging flies with Jim.

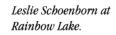

Leslie Schoenborn at Rainbow Lake.

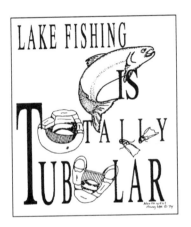

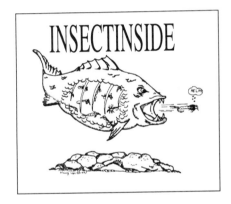

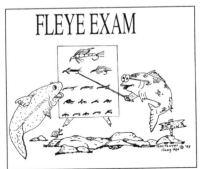

XXL = $16.50; XL, L, M = $15.00. All T-shirts are short-sleeved, light ash color, fabric is 50% cotton 50% polyester. All designs are silk screened, in color. If you want to special order a long sleeve 50/50 shirt it would be necessary to add $2.50 extra for M, Lg, XL, and $3.50 for XXL Please Indicate with LS in size box. **Please allow 3-4 weeks for delivery.**

Qty.	Size(s)	Shirt	Total
		Nature's Nymphalmaniac	
		Insectinside	
		Let's Go Fly Fishing	
		Fleye Exam	
		Lake Fishing is Totally Tubular	
		Follow The Leader	
		Total:	
		Add $3.00/Shipping & Handling:	
		Total Order:	

#1994   Please send check or money order to: **Northwest Hang Ups**
9334 SE Hillcrest Rd., Portland, OR 97266

Name: _____

Address: _____

City: _____ State: _____ Zip: _____

XXL = $16.50; XL, L, M = $15.00. All T-shirts are short-sleeved, light ash color, fabric is 50% cotton 50% polyester. All designs are silk screened, in color. If you want to special order a long sleeve 50/50 shirt it would be necessary to add $2.50 extra for M, Lg, XL, and $3.50 for XXL Please Indicate with LS in size box. **Please allow 3-4 weeks for delivery.**

Qty.	Size(s)	Shirt	Total
		Nature's Nymphalmaniac	
		Insectinside	
		Let's Go Fly Fishing	
		Fleye Exam	
		Lake Fishing is Totally Tubular	
		Follow The Leader	
		Total:	
		Add $3.00/Shipping & Handling:	
		Total Order:	

#1994   Please send check or money order to: **Northwest Hang Ups**
9334 SE Hillcrest Rd., Portland, OR 97266

Name: _____

Address: _____

City: _____ State: _____ Zip: _____

Go to laweene lake for
fermented _fish_! check it in Bowl

Fish from
here
AND
Cast
into
shorn
Bu...

FALL — (Dry Fly
calibatice at RAMY

Fish from
here

Spray/stay ← (while minnow
swmmr — Silver Body
                stay fast its po...